SABRINA FISHER REECE

Over 50 and Still Fine Looking to Date Again

The Humor, Healing, and Headaches of Midlife Dating

In59Seconds Publishing Co

First published by In59Seconds Publishing 2026

First edition

ISBN: 978-1-971622-15-6

This book was professionally typeset on Reedsy. Find out more at reedsy.com

This book is dedicated to every man and woman over fifty who still believes in love, growth, and connection. To those who have lived, learned, healed, and refused to harden their hearts, may these pages remind you that it is never too late to choose joy, clarity, and meaningful companionship.

Contents

Preface

Dating after fifty is not for the faint of heart.

By this stage in life, you are no longer dating for validation, excitement alone, or the thrill of being chosen. You are dating with experience, wisdom and discernment. You now have emotional receipts, and if we are being honest, you are dating with a much lower tolerance for nonsense.

This book was not written from a place of resentment or regret. It was written from reflection and the laughter that came *after* the tears. It was written from lessons learned the hard way and clarity earned through time, healing, and self-awareness. Over fifty does not mean over love, over desire, or over romance. It means over confusion, emotional chaos, and relationships that cost more than they give.

In these pages, I share real stories from my own journey back into dating. Some are funny. Some are frustrating and many are deeply emotional. But all of them are honest. They are not meant to shame men or glorify women, but to illuminate patterns, emotional blind spots, and the ways we sometimes abandon our own wisdom for connection.

This is also a book about emotional control. Not the kind that suppresses feelings or hardens the heart, but the kind that allows you to pause, observe, and choose yourself. Dating can trigger old wounds, insecurities, and habits we thought we had outgrown. The real work is learning how to respond differently when those moments arise.

You will meet men and women who are charming but inconsistent, generous but unavailable, confident but emotionally immature. You may even recognize versions of yourself in these stories. That recognition is not meant to embarrass you. It is meant to free you.

Healing does not mean you stop desiring love. It means you stop negotiating your peace to get it. Humor becomes your ally. Boundaries become your strength. Discernment is now your superpower.

If you are over fifty and still fine, this book is your reminder that your worth has not expired. Your heart is not naïve, it is seasoned. You are not asking for too much, you are asking the right questions, and love, real love, does not require you to abandon yourself to receive it.

Welcome back to dating.

Let's do it wiser this time.

1

No More Fixer-Uppers

I have been in many unfavorable relationships. So many, in fact, that by the time I reached my fifties, I had become a strict, no-nonsense dater. I was no longer interested in mystery, maybes, or potential. I had paid my dues, and I was determined not to repeat old mistakes.

By then, my first dates came with an interview. Not because I was bitter, but because I wanted to be abundantly clear if I chose to move forward.

I asked every question a woman could possibly think to ask a man on a first date. Are you married? Are you living with a woman? Do you still live with your mother? Do you have a girlfriend? How many children do you have? Are you actively involved in their lives? Are you driving a woman's car? Do you have your own place to live? Is your divorce officially final? Are you currently employed? Are you an ex-convict? Are you drug-free? Are you gay, straight, or other? Do you believe in a higher power?

I was not trying to be difficult. I was trying to be wise, and I was determined to avoid the pain and suffering that inevitably comes with dating the wrong man. Initially I was always dating to marry but the older I got I no longer was sure if I even wanted marriage again. I had been legally married twice and engage a few additional times. Now that I was getting older and settling into a life with assets and no debt, I was not sure I wanted to legally attach myself to a man. In my fifties a stable long term relationship that did not lead to marriage was OK with me.

However there were a few thing I could not compromise on. I could not for the life of me even begin to understand any man over 50 not having his own place. Being able to provide a stable rook over your head should not even be in question at the second half of life. You would actually be surprised how many men I encountered who were excited and determined to date but they did not have their own place.

As far as I am concerned, that makes you un-datable. Many of them did not agree but how does one feel you are eligible to date a nice woman or man and you do not even have a place of your own? Trust me I do not mean to be judgmental but priorities must be put in order.

In this book I share many of the experiences I have had while dating in my fifties. I share the good the bad and the ugly lol, so brace yourself. hopefully the stories I share may help someone save time and learn lessons.

Dating should be a fun carefree experience. It should not cause you stress of any kind. I quickly adapted to the new modern form of internet dating. A lot of people think you have to be desperate to internet date but that is not true. It's quick and easy and puts you in contact with people you may have never met before. I have signed up for many internet dating websites in the past like: Black People Meet, Plenty Of Fish and some I can't even remember.

✦

One day I got bored and re-installed my POF (Plenty of Fish) app. I do not like to waste a lot of time going back and forth on the internet, so I usually ask to exchange numbers quickly. That is exactly what I did this day. I connected with a guy named Ron. He was 57, tall and had a nice face. He also lived locally because that is a requirement of mine. I need attention so I must have a man that is local.

In our first conversation I ran off all my normal list of questions which always begins with conformation that they are fully and completely single. Not legally separated or involved in a "It's Complicated" situation. I have gotten caught up in several situations like that before but it was not because I didn't ask. You truly do not expect men over 50 to be still running around here lying.

So I asked Ron all the questions and everything seemed OK. During our second conversation. I asked him when was his last date? He told me some crazy story about being in the process of shipping his vehicle to California so he had not been on a date because he didn't have a car and was trying to raise, Yes he said raise $600 to have he car shipped to town.

I swear I try my best not to judge and I am always respectful but I do ask questions that most people wont ask. I asked if "Don't you think it is not a great time for you to focus on dating" I mean raising that $600 to get his car shipped here should be his first priority as far as I am concerned. I'm telling yall, I was very soft spoken, on purpose with the question. however he did not like being asked that. He responded with "She that is exactly what I always heard about women in California, you are gold diggers." I chuckled to myself but did not respond. However the old me, the less mature me would have let him have it. He said a

3

few more things that I tuned out once I realized he was actually mad. Once he paused from his rant I politely said "I wish you the best but I am positive we aren't a good fit". he started cursing and I hung up and blocked him.

What the heck is going on when a fifty seven year old man is that darn sensitive and had absolutely no control over his emotions. How are you even capable of getting that angry at a woman you have never met and have only spoke to twice on the phone? No thank you buddy.

Honestly there are indeed compromises woman are willing to make and many women may not even care if a man over fifty does not have a vehicle. But explosive behavior at that age is unacceptable. We do silly things when we are younger. We scream, holler and make bad decisions but once we are over fifty we should have enough wisdom to do better.

✦

There was a time in my early fifties when I dated a man named Jeff. He was handsome, and I liked him initially. We spoke on the phone five times a day, which was excessive but fun in the beginning. He laughed a lot on the phone, which I loved. He was a fifty-five-year-old man who seemed pleasant on the surface. I tried to not let the fact that he lived with his mother bother me. He smiled often and was very attentive, which was a quality I appreciated. However, his behavior was mildly erratic, and he made big issues out of very small situations. I ignored the red flags because I was excited about dating someone I liked.

One day we had a misunderstanding on the phone about something I honestly cannot even remember. I am not proud of it, but I hung up on him. I do not deal well with argumentative men. He immediately began calling me repeatedly until I answered. He asked me where I was. I was at the Inglewood Senior Center, a place I frequented for yoga, meditation, and line dancing classes. Moments later, he walked through the door.

I found it strange, but I greeted him with a smile. He asked if there was somewhere we could talk, so I took him to an outside patio. That is when he unleashed his anger. He was furious about the phone conversation and enraged that I had hung up on him. I immediately apologized for hanging up, because I was wrong, but the level of anger he displayed did not match the situation. Explosive, unpredictable behavior scares me. It went against my better judgment, but somehow I moved past it, even though that red flag was waving loudly.

He had taken me on a couple of successful dates, but one time he scheduled a date for the following day at four o'clock. The next day came and went, and he called me casually without mentioning the missed date at all. At first, I hesitated to bring it up because I had already seen how irrational his reactions could be. Still, I did not want him to believe that behavior like that was acceptable. When I asked what happened and why he did not keep his word, he raised his voice, became angry, and began screaming at me. That was the moment I was done.

The younger, more insecure version of myself would have struggled to walk away. Fear of being alone or unloved would have kept me attached to someone unstable. By this point in my life, those emotional wounds had healed. I told him it was over and wished him well. Jeff did not take it gracefully. He began sending insulting texts, attempting to belittle me and listing the names of other women he claimed treated him better. He became someone completely different, and I knew I had made the right decision.

I felt proud of myself. I had outgrown the broken little girl who would have tolerated emotional chaos and tried to fix a man. Love does not erupt in rage. Love does not scream. Love does not punish. Love is patient, respectful, and emotionally safe.

This experience reinforced an important lesson about emotional control, especially in dating. When a person cannot regulate their emotions, they will eventually try to regulate yours. Explosive reactions, unpredictability, and intimidation are not signs of passion. They are warnings. No amount of attraction or charm justifies emotional instability.

Women must learn to observe behavior without immediately excusing it. Chemistry can cloud judgment, but emotional maturity demands clarity. When someone shows you who they are in moments of conflict, believe them the first time. Do not let loneliness, excitement, or nostalgia override your intuition.

Controlling your emotions does not mean suppressing them. It means responding with wisdom instead of reacting from fear. It means walking away from chaos instead of trying to calm it. Peace is not boring. Stability is not dull. Healthy love does not leave you confused, anxious, or afraid to speak.

Every relationship is an opportunity to practice emotional discipline. Choosing calm over chaos, boundaries over attachment, and self-respect over familiarity is how we protect our hearts. When you control your emotions, you gain the power to choose love that nurtures you, not love that drains you.

✦

In August of 2023, I began dating a man who was well known in my town for his funeral business. He had sought me out on Facebook for months. He was persistent and very polite and patient. Because it took me a long while to respond to him.

Eventually, I noticed, and responded.

We met right away, and just like I always did, I asked my normal questions. He told me he was one hundred percent single. He explained that his wife had filed for divorce after many years of marriage and she also had recently passed away. I Googled him and found a actual divorce decree record online, which made me feel comfortable moving forward and go on a date with him.

We dated openly and publicly. We took pictures together every time we saw each other. We went to restaurants, held hands, snuggled close, and moved through the world like two unattached adults getting to know each other. I had no reason to doubt anything he said. On time we were at the Red Lobster and a co-worker of his walked in. They came over and greeted us both, shook his hand and we all conversation for a brief minute. This felt like further confirmation that this man was indeed single and available.

As time went on I was slightly annoyed that he worked so much and had to cancel a date or two, but everything else seemed fine. He was attentive and very complimentary. He called and texted daily. He was generous and paid for the dates. So on the surface, there were no red flags waving.

Until one day. While casually scrolling through his Facebook, I noticed a woman he had tagged in a picture from many years earlier. I was curious, so I clicked on her profile, assuming she was his sister, daughter, or perhaps the deceased wife he had mentioned. She was none of those things. She was his wife, his current wife. She was alive and well and very much still married to him. I was stunned.

Who dates another woman openly, going to restaurants, holding hands, kissing in public locally, while still married? At this point in my life, I was a successful business owner, a best-selling author, and a motivational speaker. I was a well-respected woman in the Los Angeles community. He had no right to put me in that position. I would have never chosen to share my time, energy, or body with a married man. I would never have intentionally paraded around town with someone's husband.

Now, I'm no fool. I know this happens every day. But I truly believed that I had asked enough questions for this to never happen to me, especially at this late stage in life, armed with all my over-fifty wisdom. Well I was wrong. Some people are just selfish and they want it all. Situations like this have a way of making you question yourself. They make you wonder what you're doing to attract these types of people.

I had done years of mental, emotional, and spiritual work. I had fifty-four years of life experience. Yet still, I found myself face-to-face with deception. I had to ask myself how that was even possible.

When I confronted Mr. Funeral Man, he took no accountability whatsoever. He offered a weak apology that i forced out of him and showed no real remorse. Instead, his ego took over. He became angry, angry at me for discovering the truth, and that pissed me off.

The situation escalated quickly. He began harassing me to the point where I had to file a police report. When I shared my experience with a mutual friend, it enraged him even more. Someone claiming to be his relative contacted me with threats, reminding me they knew where I lived and worked. Yes this grown ass man was now having a tantrum because I spoke up about what her did.

I wasn't afraid, but I was smart enough to protect myself. I guess I was supposed to tuck my tail and disappear quietly. But

I was so mad. Dating in your fifties is not supposed to look like this. You expect people to have worked through this level of immaturity long before now. It was unnecessary, reckless, and exhausting, and yes, I'm still mad about it. For a long time, I struggled to find the lesson in all of this. But I firmly believe that every situation, good or bad, carries a lesson meant to help us evolve.

Maybe the lesson wasn't about him at all. Maybe the lesson was that I am no longer a fixer-upper woman. I expect grown men over fifty to have gotten all of this out of their system. Crazy part is this man was not very attractive and I was proud of myself for not judging him on that. Listen I know cheating is not new and our parents, grandparents many generations before have dealt with it but if I can help it, I will not.

I no longer feel responsible for other people's healing, honesty, or accountability. I so not need closure from people who refuse to take responsibility. I don't need their apologies in order to move on. Just because some is over fifty does not mean they have morals and integrity. I had to accept a hard truth: I have absolutely no control over how other people behave, respond, or grow. I can only control my own reactions. I can choose peace, even in situations that could easily turn ugly.

As I write this, I'm still not completely certain what the full purpose of this experience was. But I do know this: I handled it differently than I would have years ago. I protected myself. I walked away. I chose clarity over chaos, and that alone tells me I have grown.

Unfortunately, we are only in charge of our own growth. We cannot force others to heal, mature, or tell the truth. But we *can* decide who no longer gets access to us. That is why this chapter is called **No More Fixer-Uppers**.

Because love is not a rehabilitation program, and I'm not accepting broken behavior as a project ever again.

2

Do Not Let Dating Affect Your Self-Esteem

By the time I reached fifty, I had been married twice. Once at age nineteen to Mr. Reece, who was a great young love of mine and the man whose last name I still carry, even though we have been apart for many years. Clearly, that one left a permanent souvenir. The second time was at age thirty-eight to a man I also loved dearly. Cody was a funny, family-man type of guy who adored me, love to dance and sing but other circumstances prevented me from staying in that marriage, and love alone, as it turns out, does not fix everything.

In my fifties, I would sometimes slow down and realize that I wanted to be in a romantic relationship again. Those marriages had happened when I was younger, during a season when I was still working through issues that were not exactly helpful for sustaining a successful marriage. At that time, I did not really know how to love or how to allow myself to be loved in a healthy way.

After years of growing up, doing extensive transformational work on myself, and learning a few lessons the hard way, I finally felt ready to experience love again. When that feeling hit, I would beeline to an online dating site, full of hope and optimism. Unfortunately, about ninety percent of the people you meet online will completely waste your time, and there will be no chemistry or connection of any kind. This is not tragic if you understand that it is part of the process and that meeting someone with the qualities you desire is still possible. Online dating takes patience, emotional stamina, and a decent sense of humor.

Anyone who truly wants a suitable mate must make the time to meet in person, spend quality time, and actually get to know people. I was always open to a first date, because I believe that after that first meeting, both people know whether they have anything in common and whether they want to proceed. I never did it but many politely pretend to check their phone and plan their exit. I love food so I am going to stay for the meal no matter what lol.

Once I became healthier mentally and emotionally, the dating process changed significantly for me. I understood the importance of not forming attachments too early. I don't mean being cold, distant, or acting like you don't care. I mean recognizing that this new person you've just met should have no control over how you feel about yourself. When we are learning to love ourselves, we can misconstrue something as simple as a person not returning a phone call as a rejection. That might not be the case, they could just be busy.

Sometimes, we create an entire story in our minds, telling ourselves, "Oh, I guess they don't like me" or "Maybe I'm not pretty or handsome enough." We tear ourselves apart with thoughts of unworthiness, even though none of it is true. Even if someone decides you are not the person they want to date, it takes nothing away from you. We should never diminish our value because of someone else's actions or feelings. They have the right to their feelings, and it's okay if you aren't the person they want to date, you still hold immense worth.

Both men and women can engage in this self-criticism; I believe that there is someone for everyone. We have all seen couples who don't seem to be a good match, usually based on physical appearance alone. But we do not know those people; we do not know what they see in each other, how kind and loving they may be, or what attracted them to one another. When we judge, it's often only based on looks.

I talk a lot in my books about dating, primarily because it seems to have a significant impact on how we feel about ourselves. Whether we are male or female, we all want to be loved. We also want other people to find us attractive. In the dating world, when we encounter disappointments because someone we were dating lets us down or mistreats us, we internalize it, thinking there's something wrong with us. That simply is not true, and we do ourselves a grave injustice by allowing those thoughts into our minds. There are many reasons some romantic relationships do not work out, and there's no need to put yourself down or label yourself as the "problem.

✦

For example, when I was about fifty two I began dating a man named Danny, whom I truly liked. Our first date was amazing, and we seemed to connect well. We met for brunch at the Coffee Company in Los Angeles. I liked what I saw as soon as he walked up. He was quite complimentary of me as well. We took pictures together and had wonderful flowing conversation throughout the breakfast.. I will admit I was disappointed when he told me he had just been released from prison after twenty-five years. I honestly could not believe it. He had on a nice business shirt and a beautiful smile. Somehow I did not let that new found knowledge affect the date. In my mind I was honestly trying very hard to not let that news affect me. Maybe people can change and I was internally telling myself not to judge him, and I didn't. He asked me out on a second date a few days later.

On the second date, we made the mistake of prematurely discussing religion, a sensitive topic that requires careful handling. Although we shared many similar beliefs, it turned out that he was a hardcore judgmental Christian who still believed that God hated gay people and felt justified in banning anyone who was homosexual from his life. He spoke of having a estranged relationship with his son for that very reason. I don't agree with those teachings; they seem unloving, outdated, man-made, and contrary to my beliefs.

Fortunately, I knew better than to get into a heated religious debate, so I changed the subject and I asked him if he thought our differing beliefs would be a problem if we continued to date. He said it would not be an issue, and we ended the evening on good terms.

One thing I liked about him was that he was always available to talk on the phone early in the morning. I love calling the man in my life bright and early before I begin my day, so the next day, I called at 6:00 a.m. We spoke briefly, but he seemed quick, short, and kind of rushed me off the phone.

Now, here's the point of this story: My mind immediately fabricated a story that went something like this: "He does like me anymore because we don't agree on religious concepts. He thinks I'm too strong-minded and is no longer interested." He never said anything of the sort, and I knew better than to make such assumptions. However, even when you practice positivity, life situations can still trigger negative thoughts.

I know that the mind can run wild with things that aren't even true if we allow it. These are the moments when we need to consciously reject negative thinking, especially when there is no basis for it. As the evening came, and I still had not heard from him, more negative thoughts crept in. I started telling myself terrible things like, "SaBrina, you are getting older; you don't look as good as you thought," or convincing myself that I had run him off because I talked too much, something I'd been told my entire life. I went to bed disappointed and a little sad, allowing myself to believe that maybe the dating ship had sailed for me and I would spend the rest of my life alone.

This is an example of unnecessary, unfounded mental torment. We must stop doing this to ourselves. Even if two people decide not to continue dating for whatever reason, we should never start attacking and belittling ourselves. Even when we make mistakes in dating, we are all learning, and those mistakes don't make you unworthy and unlovable. My point is that even though I know these positive practices very well, I am still capable of letting that negative thinking train take me down the wrong track. The difference now is that I know how to recognize when I'm on the wrong mental train and hop off and get on the right one.

The next morning, I got up and looked at my phone, no text from Danny. I told myself that it was good while it lasted and that I needed to figure out what I was doing wrong to run these men off. I also comforted myself by reminding myself that he had been in prison and my friends and family would have never accepted him anyway. I accepted my fate and went on with my day. Then, about 3 hours into my morning, Danny texted me.

"Good morning, beautiful. Sorry about last night. I see you texted me. I was dead tired. I had a really long day at work, but I hope we can talk later. Have a beautiful day."

Now, whether things worked out between me and Danny is not the point. The point is that we often mentally torture ourselves with stories we create in our heads, and that needs to stop. Dating is like fishing. There will be many fish we catch and want to throw right back into the ocean immediately. Then there will be others that look, taste, and smell delicious but end up giving us indigestion and a severe stomachache. Finding the perfect mate is a process, make it fun. Don't let every failed relationship be a personal attack on your self-esteem. Enjoy meeting people, and if someone is not a fit, don't take it personally. Remind yourself that you are amazing and it's their loss. Never give up on the belief that you will reel in that perfect fish one day if that is your heart's desire.

When we are older, people often tell us that we need to compromise our standards because there are fewer people to choose from as we age. I agree with compromising slightly, but not on everything. A man who had spent twenty-five years in prison should never have been an option for me. He had years and years of reintroduction to normal society to navigate. In hindsight, I do not think I would have had a lot of patience for that.

There will be many people that we sit down to share a meal with on a first date, and halfway through the dinner we already know they are not for us. I do not believe in being rude and cutting the date short. You never know where the conversation may go. It is also an opportunity to meet a good person and possibly make a new friend. I know that is the last thing men want to hear if they like you, but I do think it is vital to always be polite. Yes, there will be a few instances in this book where I was not as polite as I should have been, but I am growing, and so will you.

The most important part of this chapter is not allowing any failed date to affect how you feel about yourself. Everybody is not for everybody, and even if you go on a date and the person never calls you again, please do not go on a self-sabotaging attack against yourself. It truly could have nothing to do with you. I have had men tell me that my expectations of them would be too high. I have been told that because I own a business and a home, I would expect them to work harder than they were willing to. They did me a favor in the end. I too have been guilty of disappearing on men without an explanation. Today's term for it is called "ghosting."

If possible, just because it is fair and because you do not know a person's state of mind, be kind enough to let someone down easy if you can. Dating is not an easy game, but if we all approach it with respect, love, honor, and integrity, maybe it can be a pleasurable experience for everyone.

As we get older, discernment becomes more important than desperation. Wanting companionship does not mean we abandon common sense or emotional safety. Standards are not walls meant to keep love out, they are filters designed to protect the life we have already worked hard to build. Compromise should never require you to ignore your intuition or dismiss the realities you know you are not equipped to manage.

There is a difference between being open-minded and being self-sacrificing. Openness allows room for growth, conversation, and connection. Self-sacrifice, when misplaced, asks you to carry burdens that were never meant to be yours. At this stage in life, love should add to your peace, not introduce chaos disguised as potential.

Dating also has a way of exposing our old wounds if we are not careful. A bad date can trigger feelings of rejection, unworthiness, or self-doubt if we let it. That is why it is so important to remember that compatibility is mutual. Someone not choosing you does not mean you were not enough, it simply means you were not aligned.

Rejection does not diminish your value, and being passed over does not erase your accomplishments. Sometimes people walk away because they recognize they cannot meet you where you are. That honesty, whether spoken or silent, is a gift. It saves you time, energy, and emotional investment that could be better spent elsewhere.

Kindness, even in disappointment, is a reflection of maturity. You never know what someone else is carrying, and how you exit a situation matters just as much as how you enter it. Offering grace does not mean you owe anyone access to you, it simply means you choose not to harden your heart in the process.

At the end of the day, dating is not about proving your worth or convincing someone to choose you. It is about alignment, timing, and mutual readiness. When you hold your standards with compassion and confidence, you create space for the kind of love that meets you where you are and honors who you have become.

3

Dating With No Expectations

When I was younger, I developed a bad habit. If I was dating a man and could tell that the relationship was not going to work out, I would strike first. I would list all the reasons I no longer liked him and tell him it was over. At the time, I thought that was how you were supposed to handle such situations. However, as the years passed, and after a bit of therapy and self-transformation, I realized that I did this to protect myself from getting hurt.

A few more years and even more therapy and self- reflection later, I understood that it was not just about protecting myself, it was also about hurting him on the way out, punishing him for the relationship not working out. As I delved further into my own personal evolution, I fully recognized that this behavior was simply cruel. I would not want anyone to list all the reasons why they no longer liked me.

As time went on a I continued to evolve as a person I got better with that. Somethings do not need to be said. Once you realize that the behavior is coming from a place of fear and hurt, it becomes easier to stop it.

✦

There was a guy named Adrian that I dated briefly after we connected on Facebook. I had actually run into him a year prior at a movie theater with a woman, so when he reached out to me, my first question was, "Where is your girlfriend?" He explained what led to their breakup, and we moved forward. He was a sweet, country-boy type of man. We had our first meet and greet at Starbucks. It was cool. That was when I realized he did not have a car and that he walked with a limp. I told myself it did not matter. He bought me coffee and a danish, and we sat and talked for an hour or so.

Over the next week, I came and sat at his job a couple of times to talk and continue to get a feel for who he was. During one of our conversations, I asked what he was doing later, and he mentioned going to rent a room down the street at a hotel. I found it strange, but he explained that he had an early shift and that his actual home was far away, so he was just going to stay on that side of town. It later came out that he was a grown, fifty-two-year-old man sharing a room with another man in a different city.

I tried very hard not to be bothered by this, but it was difficult. I am a hardworking woman, and I found myself wondering why it felt like too much to ask for a man over fifty to have something of his own. Still, I reminded myself not to judge him too quickly. Everyone's journey is different, and life does not unfold the same way for all of us. So I continued talking to him, keeping my heart open.

We arranged a proper first date. He was a sweet guy, but he seemed a little too excited. He would say things like, "I told my coworkers that I found the one." His enthusiasm was childlike and sincere, and I did not want to crush that. I was open to believing he might grow on me, and I wanted to give things a fair chance.

We talked regularly for weeks, and eventually he planned a date. Since he did not drive, I met him at the restaurant. The first issue was small but noticeable. As I walked into the restaurant, smiling and heading toward the table, he glanced up at me but never stood to greet me. That has always been a big deal for me. Still, I kept my cool, kept smiling, and jokingly said, "Boy, you better get up and act like your mama raised you right." He laughed, stood up, and gave me a hug. I smiled through it, because I am always working on myself and choosing grace when I can.

We sat down, but he had chosen a tiny booth in the bar area. He looked uncomfortable, squeezed into the seat, and I asked if he would mind if I asked the waiter for a larger booth. He was six foot two and about two hundred ninety pounds, and it just made sense. He agreed, and we moved. I sat across from him with an open mind and an open heart.

He started talking about his day at work, mostly complaining, as he often did on the phone. Trying to stay positive, I said, "It's such a blessing to have a good job these days." I genuinely meant it. He worked as head of security at a hospital, a stable job with medical and dental benefits. I reminded him of that, even though I quietly struggled to understand how that stability had not yet translated into a car or his own place.

As the conversation continued, I noticed that he had a couple of missing front teeth and severe yellow staining. I did not react or make a face. I listened. When he mentioned dental benefits, I gently asked if he had ever considered getting his teeth fixed. I know now that I probably should have left it alone, but the door felt open. I was soft-spoken and kind with my question. He told me he was afraid of the dentist.

That moment made me reflect on something deeper. Women put an incredible amount of pressure on themselves to look nice. We worry about our weight, our hair, our clothes. Before a date, we think carefully about what to wear, not because we are insecure, but because we care. We want to show effort. We want to present ourselves well. I believe it is fair to want that same level of consideration in return.

I want to be clear that I am not hard to please. I am not looking for perfection. But some things are simply difficult to overlook. I am an extremely passionate woman who loves affection and loves to kiss. I take care of myself. I brush, floss, and make sure my smile reflects the love and attention I am willing to give. It is not unreasonable to expect a grown man to care about the mouth he will eventually want to kiss you with.

As I get older, I am willing to compromise in ways I never would have years ago. I have softened. I have grown. But there are still basics that matter. Manners. Hygiene. A sense of personal responsibility. These are not shallow expectations. They are foundations. Wanting those things does not make me unkind. It simply means I know the kind of relationship I am capable of building, and I honor myself enough to require a solid starting point.

I have no problem dating without expectations of where a relationship is going initially, but I do have expectations when it comes to the simple basics. A man having his own place, reliable transportation, basic manners, and good hygiene feels less like a wish list and more like a starting point. Come on now, am I really wrong for that? Wanting stability does not mean I am demanding perfection. It simply means I respect the life I have built and the effort I put into taking care of myself.

Dating without expectations does not mean dating without standards. It means showing up open-hearted, curious, and present, while still honoring what makes me feel safe, respected, and comfortable. With that understanding, I learned how to step into dating without expectations, but never without self-respect.

I am a hopeless romantic at heart and usually my goal was to date men who I thought
I would marry one day but as I continued to run into men that were far from eligible it became easier to date for a while without expectations of marriage. Giving a man a second chance at a second date even though initially I may not have found him attractive or there may have been some deal breaker personality traits I identified on the first date. But eventually I found dating without expectations easier. Maybe he does not have to be husband material initially. Do we know who people truly are from a first or second date anyway?

✦

There were some people in my life that I dated with absolutely no expectations, mostly because they had personality traits that I already knew were not good for me in the long run. Meaning, they were not someone I could ever see myself married to. One in particular was an older man named Black. We bonded over the death of one of my Godmothers. The crazy part is that before she passed, she told him directly, to his face, to leave me alone when she saw he was trying to get close to me. Bottom line, he did not listen. He helped me emotionally through her funeral, and somewhere along the way I realized we had great passion. The kind of magnetic chemistry that usually looks exciting on the outside but is really only good for great sex.

He was a man of many hats. We were part of the same organization, and he held prestigious titles. Although we were both single, I never wanted others to know that we were involved because Black was a force to be reckoned with, and I knew he could never be my man full time. I also did not want the other men in the organization to label me as his and stay away from me. So other than a couple of people close to me I tried to keep our involvement a secret. But discretion was not his strength. We would be at events and he would randomly grab me and kiss me in front of everyone, as if subtlety was optional. He was older than me, by how much I never knew because he refused to tell me.

What I did know and love about him was that he was smart, and we had so many intense intellectual conversations, which I absolutely loved. We also had very intense sex, once even inside a mortuary, yes do not judge us lol. His personality was all alpha, and on top of that he was an old school triple OG from back in the day. That roughneck was still very much alive inside of him. Yes, it turned me on, it made for great sex, and that we definitely had for years, but you cannot make a regular everyday relationship out of that kind of energy.

We actually expressed great love for each other, meaning we said "I love you" often, but every encounter with him was explosive and exhausting. Sometimes he would randomly curse me out in the middle of a conversation with no warning at all. We would slap and grab on each other in ways that many people would definitely consider violent, then turn around and go to sweet little dinners when our organizations had their annual conferences. His voice was deep and authoritative, and he could not always turn it off, even when the moment clearly called for softness. Physically we were very compatible. He was kind to me in his crazy gangsta way, if that makes since. I don't regret one minute of the time i spent with him.

I was involved with Black for over four years, and eventually it faded out. The love never faded but I could not focus on finding someone I could be with full time while still riding that roller coaster with him. He was an all consuming force. It was fun but it took so much out of me physically and emotionally, but I loved him dearly and I will always love him. Still, no sir, he could never have been my full time man. Which is why I was able to date him for so long without expectations. He tapped into a side of me that I was actively trying to evolve from. When I think of him and his new girlfriend, I sometimes wonder how she has the energy for the crazy gangsta side of him, because I know exactly what comes with that package. I wish them the best.

The point of this chapter is this: yes, we should know what we want for the long haul when we date, but that knowledge does not have to become pressure. Dating does not always need an agenda, a timeline, or a destination attached to it. Things should be allowed to flow, unfold, and progress naturally into a relationship if that is where they are meant to go. If they do not, but you genuinely like and enjoy enough qualities of the person, you should be able to continue dating without feeling like the "Where is this going?" conversation has to happen.

There was a time when dating was strictly about marriage, and anything less felt like wasted time. But life looks different now, and so do we. We are older, wiser, more self-aware, and more honest about what we can and cannot offer at any given moment. Sometimes two people meet simply to enjoy each other's company, laughter, affection, and shared experiences. There is nothing wrong with that. Enjoyment does not have to come with obligation.

Dating without expectations is not about avoiding commitment. It is about removing unnecessary pressure and allowing connection to reveal itself in its own time. If two people decide they want more, they can choose that together, consciously and freely. If they do not, that does not mean the connection was meaningless. It simply means it served its purpose.

There are no more rigid rules. No more forcing outcomes. No more turning every date into a life decision. Sometimes dating can simply be about enjoying someone you like, honoring the moment you are in, and trusting that whatever is meant to grow will do so naturally.

That freedom alone can change everything.

4

Not Up for the Shenanigans

What I love about mental, spiritual, and emotional advancement is that if each person monitors how they treat others, we can create a better world.

By age 54, despite all the dating debacles I described in this book, I still wasn't ready to give up on finding a compatible mate. I wasn't sure how I felt about marriage, especially since, at this stage in my life, I had a home that would be paid off in two years, all my vehicles were fully paid for, and I had finally matured enough to resist the urge to run to the dealer for a new car and another car note. I had responsibly prepared for my children's future by creating my will and living trust, and I felt really good about that. I was open to marriage, but it wasn't at the top of my list. However, a long-term committed relationship was still something I desired.

✦

After four months of casually dating men who seemed eligible, I met a man who had many of the qualities I loved in a partner. He was tall and held many positions of power, which is always a weakness for me. He was attentive and an excellent communicator. This time, I worked really hard not to let my old habits creep in. I didn't want to start picking away at him and sabotaging the relationship before it even officially began. He was a member of the same fraternal organization as me, but in a separate jurisdiction, which was perfect. It allowed us to stay private while we built a foundation and simply enjoyed each other for as long as possible. Life had taught me that was the best option. When too many people are involved in your relationship, it can be a recipe for disaster.

This segment is less about him in particular and more about how humans, who don't control their thoughts 24/7, can slip back into negative thinking patterns even after doing a lot of work to stay positive. I noticed early on in this relationship that this man wasn't as forthcoming with compliments as I liked. We exchanged a few pictures via text, and he didn't respond with the typical "You look pretty," or similar comments that I was used to. This led me to do something I don't even believe in: asking him if he found me attractive. Luckily, he quickly responded with, "You are a very attractive woman, and I'm very interested in you." That made me happy, but it also made me realize that I needed to assess why I craved constant validation from a man.

Yes, it feels wonderful to be told you're beautiful by someone you're dating, but those compliments shouldn't have the power to lower our self-esteem when we don't receive them. I ended the relationship once I realized he was simply too busy for a girlfriend. Each interaction has a lesson in it. From that short dating experience, I learned that my self-esteem wasn't as high as I thought. So, I went to work on building a stronger, more authentic self-esteem.

I am as busy as they come. But if I am truly interested in a man I will make time for him. When men are over 50 you honestly do not expect them to be still playing the playboy game. But sometimes that is exactly what is going on. I am not sure it that was the case with this man but he definitely did not have enough time for me.

I am a member of the same organization as he is but I am not obsessed with it. Every conversation we had was some rant about the organization and how he was not being respected blah blah blah.

Even when we did go on a date he insisted on driving way across town to a restaurant of his choice. It was annoying. We took pictures all the time and he never once pulled back so I had no reason to suspect that he wasn't being honest.

✦

There was this man that I connected with after doing his hair several times. He was a Southern gentleman type. I honestly do not remember exactly how it evolved past the hairdresser and client relationship, but it did. Initially, he caught my interest because he was a great thinker and reader like me. I could mention a quote or a passage from a book, and he would already know it. That definitely intrigued me. It was so hard to find a man I could have stimulating conversations with, and that alone made him stand out.

Denell was smart, and like many of the men I seem to attract, he wore many hats. He was once a minister, a businessman who claimed to own several properties, and an old-school street hustler. He was tall, charming, and whenever he came to town, he always treated me to dinner. Years went by, and one day he called me out of the blue and told me he was in town. I was not involved with anyone at the time, so I let him come over. As usual, we talked for hours and hours. He stayed in town for a few days, and we went out to eat a couple of times. During that visit, he strangely asked if he could store his car in my backyard. I did not mind, so he brought it over, parked it, and then left town. The car sat there for months before he eventually came back to get it.

Because he was always in and out of town, I never took him too seriously. I also refrained from involving myself physically, but the door was always open for us to build something if time had permitted it. I was never rushing the situation.

Once, I attended a Lisa Nichols seminar in San Diego, California, and he decided to come join me. I did not mind at all. He drove down and met me for lunch. I did not think anything of it when he asked for my room number. Later, when I checked out, I realized he had charged his sixty-dollar parking fee to my room. Yes, he had always taken me to dinner and had been very generous in that way, but this time he did it without saying a word. I noticed it, but I let it go.

The following year, I attended the Toastmasters International Conference in Washington, D.C. When he found out I was there, he hopped on a plane to come visit me. This was during my early days as a motivational speaker, so I was not about to miss a day of the conference running around the city with him. He bought his own ticket and joined me at the speech competitions. In our spare time, we toured Washington, D.C. together. We got along very well. We were affectionate, communicated easily, and enjoyed each other's company.

One day, we went on a bus tour of the city and somehow got separated. When I finally made my way back to the bus, I was alarmed to find him sitting calmly in his seat instead of looking for me. I probably overreacted, but I was furious. I need a protector in my life. Why was he sitting comfortably instead of frantic and searching for me? That night, we argued for hours because he could not see my point. At that time in my life, I was not yet my calm, peaceful self.

The next day, I decided to fly home early and leave him there. That made him angry. My flight was at eight in the morning, and his was not until eleven that night. He asked if he could stay in my hotel room until he left for the airport. I could not bring myself to agree. I remembered how he had charged his parking to my room in San Diego without telling me. I did not feel comfortable leaving him alone in a room under my name with an open tab. I left for the airport and called the front desk to officially check out, letting them know the room was vacant and ready for resale. He was furious. He wanted to stay in the room all day under my name. That moment marked the end for us. Things never went any further after that.

A year or so later, he called and told me he had lost everything due to bad business investments. I wished him well, and we never spoke again.

What I learned from that experience stayed with me. Just because a man shows up and pays for dinners does not mean he is who he says he is. Sometimes we take people at their word, and quite often the claims about owning businesses, properties, and assets are not even true. The truth is, it has never been a requirement of mine for a man to own property or be wealthy. But honesty is non-negotiable.

There is a woman who is okay with the truth. There is a woman who can handle where a man really is in life. But once a person is dishonest with me or tries to take advantage of me, I can never see them the same way again. At that point, I am always on alert.

I am not up for the shenanigans at all.

This chapter is not about money, status, or appearances. It is about discernment. It is about paying attention to patterns, not just promises. We need to understand that consistency matters more than charm, and integrity matters more than presentation.

As women, we must stop confusing presence with protection and generosity with character. Showing up is important indeed, but how someone behaves when you are not watching tells you far more. When small boundaries are crossed, they are rarely small accidents. They are signals that you should not ignore.

The lesson here is simple but powerful. Listen to what people do, not just what they say. Honor your intuition when something feels off. Remember that walking away from inconsistency is not a loss, it is an act of self-respect.

Now let's talk about the shenanigans many of us have encountered. By the time we reach our fifties, most of us have lived enough life to know the difference between ambition and imagination. Yet in dating, many people still present themselves as future versions they never fully committed to becoming. Dreams are not the problem. Potential is not the issue. The shenanigans begin when someone tries to sell you a résumé instead of a reality.

There is a difference between saying "this is who I am" and "this is who I plan to be." There is also a difference between vision and fantasy. If someone wants to be a business owner, the first step is starting a business, not just talking about one. If someone wants to own property, the work begins with planning, saving, and execution, not reminiscing about what they once had decades ago.

At this stage of life, history alone does not qualify someone.

What matters is what exists now. Who are you now? I have heard men proudly declare that they owned a home in their thirties, ran a company in their forties, or had wealth at one point in their lives. While those experiences may be part of their story, they do not automatically translate into stability today. Life happens, Yes I understand that, and people lose things. Circumstances change drastically at times. There is no shame in that. The issue arises when the past is used to mask the present.

If you are dating in your fifties and have no assets, no plan, and no forward movement, it is misleading to lead with who you used to be. Growth is not measured by what once existed, but by what you are actively building now.

This applies to women as well. Some women, often exhausted by financial strain or disappointed by past relationships, approach dating with an unspoken agenda. They are not looking for partnership. They are looking for rescue. They are not seeking love. They are seeking relief. While there is nothing wrong with desiring security, it becomes problematic when dating turns into a strategy for survival rather than a choice rooted in wholeness.

Dating is not meant to be a financial transaction disguised as romance. A relationship built on need instead of mutual desire will always be unbalanced. When one person is looking for a provider and the other is looking for admiration, the foundation is already unstable.

Not up for the shenanigans means being honest about where you are and what you want. It means not exaggerating accomplishments, inflating income, lying about being single, or dressing up struggle as mystery. It means not borrowing confidence from imagined futures or past achievements. It means showing up as you are, with clarity, accountability, and truth. Trust me there is someone who will date you right where you are.

True confidence does not need to impress others. It does not need to brag or convince. Confidence is calm and consistent. It is open, transparent and honest.

Another common shenanigan is emotional storytelling designed to rush intimacy. Trauma bonding, oversharing, and premature vulnerability are often mistaken for connection. While openness is important, dumping unresolved pain onto someone you barely know is not intimacy. It is emotional bypassing.

People who have not done their inner work often try to bond through shared wounds instead of shared values. They speak in absolutes and they move too fast. They mirror your desires and they tell you exactly what you want to hear. This is not alignment. It is performance.

Discernment requires slowing down, taking your time and asking quiet questions and watching how someone lives, not how they speak. It requires noticing whether words and actions align over time. We must resist the urge to fill in gaps with hope.

Another shenanigan is selective honesty. People tell you the truth in pieces, revealing information only when necessary, hoping you are already emotionally invested by the time the full picture emerges. They may not lie outright, but they omit, minimize, and reframe. Clarity is always fuzzy and accountability is avoided.

When someone truly respects you, they do not gamble with your time. At this stage of life, time is one of our most valuable assets. We are no longer here to babysit potential, decode inconsistency, or tolerate confusion. We are here for reciprocity. We are here for emotional safety and honesty, even when it is uncomfortable.

Not up for the shenanigans also means taking responsibility for our own behavior. It means not ignoring red flags because we are lonely. No longer excusing behavior because we want the story to end differently this time. It means we stop romanticizing struggle or mistaking chaos for passion.

Maturity in dating looks like restraint and patience. It resembles curiosity without attachment. Your standards are not rigid. It means being open without being available to nonsense.

The truth is, many people are not dishonest because they are malicious. They are dishonest because they are unsure of themselves. They want to be more than they are, but they have not yet done the work to become that person. Compassion allows us to understand that, but wisdom allows us to walk away anyway.

You do not need to judge someone harshly to choose differently. Discerning is not shaming. It is simply deciding that your life, your peace, and your future deserve more than that. You are not obligated to stay in confusion to prove you are kind. Kindness includes being kind to yourself. You matter most.

This chapter is a reminder that dating later in life is not about proving anything. It is about alignment. It is about choosing partnership over performance. It is about reality over illusion. At this stage of our live we need peace and security.

When someone tells you who they are, listen. When a person shows you where they are, believe them. Do not negotiate with potential that has no proof of effort. Do not accept stories in place of substance.

You are not up for the shenanigans anymore because you have already lived through enough lessons to recognize them, and that is not being harsh.

That is being wise.

5

Control Your Emotions

✦

On May 30, 2024 my patience with dating was running very low. So low that after making contact with a guy named Billiam on Facebook dating I told him to meet me right now. I had no desire to waste time bonding with him for even one day if we were not compatible. Surprisingly he agreed and we met on Florence at a place I frequent called "Tals Cafe."

He was tall and greeted me with a very nice and welcoming smile and a pleasant attitude. Breakfast was great. We bonded emotionally after sharing a few life stories. One being the death of his mother only a few weeks earlier. He understandably got emotional at breakfast and I was able to comfort him and share some heartbreaking losses of my own.

We quickly became an exclusive couple and things were great. He was attentive which I loved initially. He opened every door and paid every bill. We blended well together. He was welcoming and very generous with my children. He had a great sense of humor. As the months flew by some of his attentive behavior became annoying. Things like wiping my mouth after every meal and deciding when I was thirsty and literally putting a cup up to my mouth, that I didn't ask for, because he felt I was thirsty.

People thought I had found the perfect man. He loved the camera and didn't mind performing with me and my daughter in our Instagram and TikTok videos. He never said no to anything. He was open and verbal to everyone about his love for me. It was cute at first. But I quickly learned that balance is needed in all areas. Too much affection can be a nuisance.

We went on many outings together and had a lot of fun. Whatever I wanted to do and wherever I wanted to go, he was willing and ready. I was not great at planning things on his own but he had no problem complying to my ideas. Eventually I realized he had no hobbies or passions of his own. No desires , no dreams or goals. Not one positive relationships with friends or family at all. He spoke negatively about both ex-wives and bragged about frequently severing relationships with friends and family, which bothered me terribly. I would try to introduce my positive outlook on life to him and he always seemed receptive but it wasn't who he was. He seemed to truly want to be a better person but found it easier to act the part rather than actually do the work needed to authentically become a better person.

I have to give him a little credit, Billiam seemed to truly desire to be a kinder human being. When I suggested books for his to read, he would actually read them. He also read two of my books cover to cover. Which greatly impressed me. He was a alpha male with a deep voice. He had been living in Texas for 20 years but was originally from California.

I enjoy being in a relationship but I also have grown to love myself so much that I equally enjoy spending time alone. He never tired of me. He always wanted my full attention which started to make me feel smothered. He taught me how to play pool and spades so I began having card parties at my home.

We were in our fourth month of dating in September 2024. This particular card party was the largest I had so far. There were about twelve people there, four of which were children. At previous parties I told him he had been a little too aggressive with my friends and family during the card games. A lot of people slap cards and dominoes on the table when they play games like that but his antics were extreme and came with ridicule of each players skills. He had a real deep voice and a dominant demeanor. According to him he had forty years experience playing cards and he was the only expert in the room. That arrogant attitude began to annoy everyone in the room.

I had been asking God why I didn't seem to have strong feelings for this man being that he seemed to possess many of the qualities I desired in a man. He was attentive ,affectionate, always available and extremely financially generous. However my heart just wasn't in it. We verbally told each other we loved each other but I truly hadn't gotten there yet. I know what love felt like and this was not it. I stayed because I was open to growing with him and hopeful of stronger feelings developing but they honestly never did. So by September I was already ready to end the relationship. He had begun having some physical health challenges that made him insecure as a man. That caused him to be even more clingy which I hated.

I do believe people come into our lives for a reason. I frequently asked God, "Why did this man come into my life and why can't I bring myself to fall in love with him.?" There was something about the way he treated other people that bothered me. He was kind, loving and generous with me and my daughters but to everyone else in the world he was cruel and dismissive. It bothered me a lot and I thought it quite unusual that only my kids and I got to see a happy, loving man. If this is truly who he was then why were these personality traits only shared with us. No one in his family spoke highly of him nor he of them. I found that strange as well.

It also became a concern of mine that he didn't seem to possess anything of his own. He said he moved back to California to take care of his dying mother during her last days. I often wondered who he was and what he had been doing all those years in Texas. He said is worked for a company called Pods for years but he didn't speak of too much else regarding his Texas life.

Yes, he spent a lot of money on me but it was money he recently acquired from his mother's estate after she passed. She passed six days before we met. I had the pleasure of sorting through her clothes and belongings to prepare her home, which he had inherited, to be sold. He planned on using the money from the sale of his mother's home and settling in California and building a life with me.

His mother's name was Arthurlean. Yes, her fathers name was Arthur. While helping him clean out her home I bonded with her even though we never met. We were a lot alike. She was a hard working woman who retired from the L A Times after 30 years. She raised two children and purchased a nice home for them. She seemed to be a "make it happen by any means" type of woman like me. She loved cowboy style clothing just like me. I wore a pair of her cowboy boots to an event that he and I attended. I longed to have known her. There were so many similarities between his mother and I that I started to believe I was supposed to meet her son and indirectly connect with her even though she was not alive. I believed she would have loved me.

Billiam, on the other hand, appeared to have been broke and possibly destitute at sixty-one had his mother not passed away. All the money he used to wine and dine my children and I with was money he gained access to after her passing. That does not devalue the money itself, but when a man is talking about marriage, I need to understand his long-term earning potential. I needed to know what his plan had been while living in California.

I am not the type of woman who would ever move a man into a home with me and my daughters, so I began asking questions about long-term plans. It quickly became clear that he was finished working and intended to live off the money his mother left him. While that is not impossible for someone with strong business sense, his thinking did not reflect that level of planning. He spoke about buying homes in California and investing two hundred thousand dollars with a friend. He bragged to me and to others that he was now a millionaire.

At first, I found this amusing and entertained the idea for a while, but eventually I did the math for him. I reminded him of the cost of real estate in California and walked him through Realtor fees, closing costs, and other expenses. What would be left over did not qualify as millionaire status. By that point, I already knew I was not going to marry him, and I felt it was important for him to make realistic plans with the money, especially since he had no desire to ever work again.

I would casually ask him about his previous career and what assets he had acquired over the years, but I never pushed for answers because I did not want to seem judgmental. Many women would not have been concerned, especially since he was consistently spending money. However, I was bothered and

41

wanted to know the true character of the man he was. Who was he before his mother's death? How was he supporting himself financially before he had access to her bank accounts?

He did not appear to be a hardworking man I could build a life with. His generosity did not impress me because I knew the money came from his mother's hard work, not from anything he had built for himself.

So by September 19, 2024 the day of the final card party we gave at my home, after almost 6 months of dating. I was just about certain I was leaving the relationship soon. He made it easy by having an adult tantrum at the card party because I was not paying enough attention to him. He seemed oblivious to the many guests that were present and a witness to his childlike behavior. He stormed in and out of the house erratically. It made me and everyone in the room very nervous. I did my best to ignore his manic behavior but he kept asking to speak to me outside. The first time he asked I went outside to see what he wanted. He was angry and ranted about me not knowing the proper way to play cards. I calmly told him that if he could not refrain from being so aggressive then I no longer wanted him to teach me. He was furious. So mad that his lips began to quiver. He expressed an anger I had never seen in him before. I thought to myself "This is Over". I went back into the house to greet the new guest that had arrived and continued with the party. He had given me a cute card box that belonged to his mother. He decided to snatch the card box off the table in front of everyone and take it to his car. He exhibited unbelievable unstable behavior. I was done. I knew I would never see him after that day. I continued to play cards with my guest who kept asking me "Is everything okay". Finally he just could not control himself anymore and stood up mid card game and walked over to me and asked once again if I would come outside. I calmly replied "No". He then said "I'm leaving". I said "Okay, drive safely". Although I was very calm. I was very nervous. He is 6ft 1 and seemed totally out of control. This tapped right into my childhood triggers of witnessing my grandfather take the life of my grandmother, her husband of 32 years. However I calmly refused to come outside with him. He angrily stormed out of the door. My fear made me hop up immediately to lock the door. Everyone in the room was stunned. I truly did not know what to do. The husband of one of my friends stood up and went outside to ensure he left. He attempted to come back into the house but my friend prevented him from doing so. He left and I never spoke to him again.

I would rather be single than continue to date a man that has no control over his emotions. I knew that someone who was so cruel and spoke so badly about others' true colors would shine through eventually. I personally believe that is why I was not able to develop feelings. God was protecting me. I could feel that ticking time bomb in him just waiting to explode. I left that relationship a little confused though. He seemed so nice and joyful initially. Although the attentiveness was excessive it seemed sincere. I had to go back and assess what love actually looked like after dating him.

I realized that although I do enjoy a balanced amount of attention and affection. I don't need a man spoon feeding me and deciding when I am thirsty. There is a clear difference between love and obsessive behavior. I want a partner that has interests and hobbies of his own. I want them to have a life of their own that I can add to. I do not want to be their life. I learned a lot from the relationship. I learn to stay calm even when I am annoyed and afraid. I feel if I had not responded in the calm manner the day of the party that the situation could have been explosive. People come into our lives for a reason. This relationship taught me that all that glitters is not gold. I learned from dating him exactly what I do not want in a man.

Dating brings up emotions that broken people can't handle. Take your time and truly get to know the person. Try to ask the pertinent questions. Do not rush when getting to know someone. Inauthentic people can only keep up their farce for so long. If we all start to be honest with ourselves and others, we'll save ourselves and everyone else a lot of grief. In the end, the message I'm trying to convey is to enjoy your journey, keep learning, and stay optimistic.

We all deserve the best in life. We deserve a kind, loving companion. I love the idea of being in love, and when I date, I date with the intention of being open hearted yet wise. All connections will not be a match. Enjoy the process with no initial expectations. Loving yourself sincerely will generate a beautiful energy that will eventually draw that perfect mate to you.

✦

There was a big, dark-skinned man I met online during a time in my life when I truly cared very little about physical appearance. By that point, looks were no longer a priority for me. I was open to falling for someone based solely on inner beauty, character, and effort. In that regard, he seemed like the perfect candidate.

What initially attracted me to him was his willingness to come over and work out with me in my home gym. That mattered to me. He was very overweight, but the fact that he was willing to do something about it showed initiative and self-awareness. That alone earned my respect and openness. I was at a place in my life where I understood that bodies change, seasons shift, and perfection fades. What mattered more was effort, consistency, and intention.

Our first date was at a restaurant called The Warehouse, and it went fairly well. The conversation flowed, and while there was only a little chemistry, it felt comfortable. We went on a few more dates and even spent Christmas together. He liked to cook, so we made a few meals at my home. There still wasn't any physical chemistry, but I believed it could grow. I was intentionally giving things time, allowing connection to develop naturally instead of rushing to judgment.

One day while relaxing at home, I suddenly remembered that a storm was coming and I needed tar for a section of my roof. I jumped up, but my car was in the shop, so I asked him if he could take me to Home Depot quickly. He growled and said he was tired. I explained that rain was coming and I really needed to get the tar. I was not asking him to get on the roof or fix anything. I simply needed transportation to pick it up.

He kept repeating, "Where did that come from?" I explained that we had been busy cooking and I forgot. I even apologized for asking. He stood up with the worst attitude I had ever seen in a grown man and snatched his keys to take us. He drove us there, but his energy was nasty and hostile. I stayed quiet because my focus was getting what I needed and getting back home safely.

When we arrived at Home Depot, he sat in the car while my young daughter and I got out. I walked back to the window and politely asked if he would help carry the five-gallon bucket of tar because it was too heavy for me. He got out with the same angry, aggressive attitude. In that moment, something inside me settled. I knew I was done.

This man had just cooked in my kitchen. He had been welcomed into my home. He had shared family time with us.

Yet he was displaying resentment, irritation, and emotional volatility over a simple request. That told me everything I needed to know. Red flags are not always loud explosions. Sometimes they show up in small moments, when someone reveals how they handle inconvenience, responsibility, and basic kindness.

He drove us back home and became upset again when he realized he needed to carry the tar into the backyard. As he walked it back, I was already composing my breakup message in my head. I was grateful that all I had given him were moments, meals, and access to my home, nothing deeper. There were no emotional entanglements, no illusions left to unravel.

Once he set the tar down, I called out, "Good night, drive safely," knowing he lived about an hour away. When I went inside, I finished the breakup text I had already started and sent it. I told him clearly that I never wanted to see him again and that anyone capable of displaying that level of anger, especially around my child, was not for me. I sent the message and blocked him.

This experience taught me something important. Being open-minded does not mean ignoring red flags. Compromising on physical attraction does not mean compromising on character. As we get older, it is natural and healthy to shift our priorities. We stop chasing surface-level beauty and start valuing stability, effort, and emotional maturity. That is growth, not desperation.

However, no amount of openness should require tolerating disrespect, hostility, or emotional instability. Inner beauty is revealed through behavior, not words. Kindness shows up when someone is tired. Character reveals itself when a situation is inconvenient. Emotional safety matters more than physical attraction ever will.

I was not being mean. I was being discerning. I gave grace

where grace was appropriate, and I listened when my spirit spoke. That is the lesson. You can be compassionate without being careless. You can be open without being blind. Dating later in life is not about lowering standards. It is about refining them.

When someone shows you who they are in the small moments, believe them!

Looking back, the Home Depot incident was not the first time I had seen this side of him. There had already been a moment that unsettled me, but I chose to brush past it.

On another date at Whiskey Red's in the Marina, my daughter and I had already ordered our meals when it was his turn. He asked the waitress for a specific type of oyster, and she politely explained that they did not have it. I am always kind and respectful to servers, but his tone shifted immediately. He insisted that he needed those particular oysters, even after she clearly stated they were unavailable. He became demanding and eventually asked to speak to the cook, which felt excessive and embarrassing. The energy at the table changed, and my eight-year-old daughter was sitting right there, quietly taking it all in.

I calmly stepped in and said, "Babe, they don't have it. What would be your second choice?" He could tell by my expression that I was unhappy, not just with his treatment of the waitress, but with the emotional outburst itself. It felt like a spoiled, childlike reaction to disappointment, and it was happening in front of my actual child. I made a mental note that day, even though I did not act on it.

That memory came rushing back to me at Home Depot. His irritation, his attitude, the way he responded to a simple request, and the resentment he carried toward helping me all mirrored that earlier moment at the restaurant. These were not isolated incidents. They were patterns. Small situations consistently triggered oversize reactions, and each time, I found myself managing the discomfort rather than him managing his emotions.

By the time he angrily carried the bucket of tar into my backyard, the picture was clear. This was not about physical attraction or my willingness to compromise. This was about emotional regulation, respect, and how a man responds when something does not go his way. I realized then that the issue was never his appearance. It was his temperament, and that is something no amount of openness, patience, or grace can fix.

Red flags rarely arrive all at once. They show up in small moments, in restaurants when someone is told no, in parking lots when plans change, and in everyday situations that require patience and emotional control. When those moments are ignored, they do not disappear. They repeat, grow louder, and eventually become impossible to manage.

As women, especially as we mature, we often pride ourselves on being understanding and open-minded. We tell ourselves we are evolving when we overlook behavior that once would have stopped us immediately. But emotional stability is not something to negotiate. Kindness is not optional. Respect is not something that develops later.

Compromising on physical appearance can be an act of wisdom and growth. Compromising on character never is. A man's true attractiveness is revealed in how he manages frustration, how he treats people who cannot give him what he wants, and how safe he makes you feel in ordinary moments.

The lesson for me was firm and unmistakable. Control your emotions, and pay attention when others cannot control theirs. Peace is not earned by enduring discomfort. It is protected by walking away the first time your spirit tells you something is wrong.

6

Sexuality & Spirituality

✦

When you are on a spiritual journey, you come across many people who feed you information, and all of that information is not accurate. I once had a life coach or spiritual advisor whose main focus was teaching me to "transcend human emotion." As his student, I wasn't allowed to express hurt, pain, or fear because his theory was that in order for mankind to evolve to their higher selves (as he believed he had), they must transcend natural human emotion. I bought this hook, line, and sinker at first until I later started to become sad and disheartened with his teachings. Something didn't feel right. I was confused and in more pain than before I began working with him.

Although I knew the benefit of not allowing yourself to stay in an unhappy state, I was struggling each week in his class with having to stifle all human emotions. It just didn't feel natural. He referred to himself as "D-Amen or Di Amen De Mere." He assured his students that he had spiritually ascended to these higher levels of consciousness and self-mastery that he was teaching us and that was the ultimate goal for all humans. He promised to take me through spiritual exercises that would finally rid me of the pain and trauma of my past. I was elated and began to feel that he was sent to me by God himself to help me heal. He told me that he was the key to my complete healing and his spirit and mine had been connected in several past lives and it was destined that we eventually came together.

I had failed in all of my past efforts to heal from witnessing the tragic murder of my grandmother, who had raised me from infancy. At that point in my life, I was still suffering from the memory of that horrible incident. My grandmother was killed by a single gunshot womb to the head, in front of me, by my grandfather, her husband of thirty-two years. I was only seventeen years old when I witnessed this horrific incident. When I became a student of Mr. D-Amen's, I communicated to him my desire to finally heal from this particular past trauma. He assured me that he possessed the knowledge to help me, and through his guided meditative techniques I would finally be able to put it in my past. He even told me that during a deep meditation we would travel back to the day of the murder of my grandmother and change the outcome which would allow me to finally heal for good.

I started to believe he was the key to my healing and peace. I was hopeful and desperate and had put complete faith in this particular man who was a very attractive, physically fit, dark skinned, bald headed, muscular man whose day job was physical training. He and I would read and meditate privately together. We began to grow much closer; he even took me with him when he physically trained some of his clients. I wasn't even put off when he and I became physically involved, because he said due to our deep spiritual connection it was only natural that the next step for us was to connect sexually. There was not one ounce of suspicious doubt. I trusted that Mr. D- Amen had all the answers to my emotional problems. He had been a minister once in another state and according to him he had been trained by the most reputable kemetic teachers in the "Laws of Maat." He assured me that he and I were "Twin Flames" and had been connected in many different lifetimes or incarnations as he called them. Although that concept was foreign to me, I trusted and believed his every word. Somehow, I let his Divine self convince me that the female companion he lived with was not the woman he desired. I believed him when he said he and she had no spiritual connection and he had made a horrible mistake by allowing her to move from another state to be with him. He said he had lost his mental and physical desire for her. He told me that he must meditate on the correct, divine way to exit the relationship, so he would have favor with God. All while we continued our physical relationship.

Needless to say, I was naive for being so trusting, but I tell you this story because the urgent desire to heal from things that have hurt and haunted your life can make you very vulnerable. That kind of vulnerability can cloud your judgment. When I became involved with him, I had not yet fully understood my own power, the amazing power that God gave me to take charge of my own healing and initiate the steps I needed to put my past trauma behind me. I was still believing in a human being. I gave him the power and the control over my personal healing. Even when his actions in no way resembled the Divine Being he claimed to be, my desire for healing allowed me to dismiss the obvious deception and convince myself that the key to all my pain was in a man, this man in particular. This self-proclaimed master teacher of Maat'. I thought he could actually heal me for good. I was so excited to finally be rid of the suffering I had been living with for years. I was wrong, and that situation caused me a lot of pain and devastation. He was definitely no elevated being. I sincerely believed that God had sent this person to help me but I had to accept that he was simply the typical flawed male opportunist. That was a hard lesson, but in retrospect, with the state of mind I was in, I completely understand how I was misled by him. I take full responsibility for allowing myself to be reeled in. This was my fault. I didn't know that the only person that can truly heal me is me. God already placed within me all the tools I needed to repair my heart from all the trauma I had experienced. I know the truth now. It's all in my hands. I have the key to my own healing and happiness. God gave it to me at birth.

It turns out that he violated the rules of the spiritual unity center where we met by becoming personally involved with his student. As a result, he was suspended. I in no way blame the African spiritual center where he taught because they do not promote this type of behavior and they took immediate action to rectify it. However, I was left to undo the emotional damage and figure out how to assure it never happened again. I'm much stronger now, and due to the lesson learned, I don't regret a thing. It taught me that no human being can heal me. God gave us the tools we need, and it's time we all begin to use them, and that is specifically what I began to do. I learned to turn inward. I began sitting in silence more often and practicing longer periods of meditation. Doing so allowed me to truly figure out my own areas of self sabotage. I learned exactly what I was doing mentally to continue to suffer from my past. I learned to take complete responsibility for my own emotional advancement. There may be people that can guide us in our healing, but ultimately it is up to us and us alone.

Sometimes when we do not receive the love that we are meant to have from birth, we spend most of our lives looking for it in other people. Sometimes those people let us down. Whether we are aware of it or not, we look to them to fix the broken parts of us, because we have not yet learned to fix them ourselves. Unfortunately, I formed that type of relationship with one of my siblings. This relationship, although it was always based purely in love, it caused me to form unhealthy desires for approval. Because there were no parents in our lives. My need for validation came solely from my sibling's opinion of me. This unhealthy attachment prevented me and my sister from simply being sisters. Her maternal role in my life caused me to unfairly put her on a pedestal she never asked to be on, but it caused my disappointment in her to be intensified once I realized that she too was as flawed as I, and that she also had emotional issues to heal from. She processed our mother's abandonment completely differently than I did. She appeared much stronger than I was emotionally which caused me to lean on her for emotional support after the murder of our grandmother who raised us. I always felt that I needed to be perfect to be loved completely by her. I always had a fear of her walking away and abandoning me like our mother. After conversations where my issues were highlighted, I became extremely hurt and felt constantly attacked, which created distance in our relationship. Early on, I didn't realize how this dynamic affected me emotionally. Because I was so broken, I accepted it and tried to please so that I could be loved. I didn't have the courage or the strength to say, "I'm great," or "So what, I didn't do everything the way you would have, but I'm proud of me." I would not actually gain that strength until much later in my life. When I finally did, it felt wonderful.

No one deserves to feel less than anyone else. We are all amazing blessings from God. Transforming the belief that we are not as worthy as others is up to us. People will hurt and disappoint us. Most of the time they are not intentional acts. Many will go to their graves never understanding the full extent of the pain they have caused us. You have to choose not to suffer. You have to choose to forgive them whether they ask for your forgiveness or not. Learn to love the best in them even when they point out what they feel is the worst in you.

Everyone reacts and responds to others based on their own beliefs and history, which helps them form their individual perceptions of how life should be. I know beyond a shadow of a doubt that my sister loves me and has never meant me any harm. However, sometimes people can unconsciously inflict their perception of the world onto others, which can cause them great pain. Their idealistic view of the world can be forced onto others all in the name of love.

✦

One day my kids and I were at the neighborhood market called Buddha Market. I sent my daughters into the store to grab a few groceries. As they were walking out, I noticed an older gentleman following them. I immediately panicked and jumped out of my car. I was looking at him crazy when my older daughter spoke up and told me he had just paid for their groceries. Suddenly my death stare turned into a kind smile, and I thanked him for buying our food.

I still wasn't completely convinced that he wasn't attempting to talk to my daughter, who was in her very early twenties. I said, "Whew, I'm relieved, because I thought you were following my daughter out of the store to get her number." He laughed and said, "No, I was just being a nice guy, plus I'm old enough to be her grandfather." We both laughed. I gave him my business card and told him that if he ever needed a little daily motivation, he could look up my videos on YouTube.

He texted me almost immediately and asked to take me on a breakfast date. I agreed, and the next morning I met him at IHOP. Initially, I was taken aback by his very colorful outfit, but of course I smiled and gave him a big hug.

We sat down to eat, and he had a larger midsection and had to struggle a bit to get into the booth. I honestly don't mind a little stomach on a man. He was quite short, but once again, I kept an open mind. I thanked him again for purchasing our groceries, and he went on to say that he was a very generous man. He told me he used to sing in a group similar to The Temptations. I googled it when I got home, but maybe I spelled it wrong because I couldn't find anything.

Once we were done eating, he walked me to my car and was a little more affectionate than I prefer on a first date. He tried to plant a big, juicy kiss on my lips, but I backed away just in time. I enjoy affection, but that was too much and far too soon.

After that, he began sending the typical morning, noon, and evening "Good morning, beautiful" texts. I am someone who can only deal with that for so long. What's next, sir? You are not about to "good morning, beautiful" me to death. I am a woman who needs plans. Meaning, plan a second date or stop communicating. I can take charge when necessary, but I am old school. Initially, I need a man to initiate the first two dates.

Months passed, and I just couldn't take it anymore. So I finally asked, "Would you like to see me again?" He said, "Absolutely." Then I asked, "Well, why haven't you asked me out?" He responded that all of his money was tied up in his investments. If I had five dollars for every time I heard that, I would definitely be rich. While I don't mind paying for a date, I was not willing to do it this early in the game.

Early one morning he tried to switch it up, and his text read, "How is my chocolate sexy this morning?" I could not have been more annoyed. I told him I had met someone else and was no longer interested. I sent my "wish you the best, God bless you" farewell text and moved forward.

This man was sixty years old. I refused to keep asking a grown man when the next date would be. I am starting to believe that some men feel they score a lot of points with the first date and then never have any intention of arranging or paying for a second one. My brain does not even understand how you move forward without dating. Why are we still texting daily? In my mind, it has to be going somewhere. That somewhere does not necessarily have to be a committed relationship, but the momentum must keep progressing to keep interest alive.

What I learned from this experience is that consistency without intention is meaningless. Daily texts without direction create confusion, not connection. Words alone do not build attraction, safety, or trust. Effort does. Planning and action does.

At this stage of my life, I am not looking to be entertained by empty communication. I am looking to be pursued with clarity and respect. If a man is interested, it should be evident in how he shows up, how he plans, and how he invests his time and energy. Interest without follow-through is not interest at all.

I am also no longer impressed by generosity that lacks structure. Buying groceries or paying for one breakfast does not establish leadership or readiness for partnership. Real generosity shows up in consistency, accountability, and the willingness to move things forward.

I refuse to shrink my standards to make someone else comfortable. I will not carry the momentum of a connection by myself. Relationships require mutual effort, and dating is not something that should feel stagnant, confusing, or one-sided.

Texting is not dating. Attention is not intention, and affection without direction is just noise.

I know what I want, and I am no longer afraid to walk away from what does not align. Clarity is attractive. Boundaries are powerful. At this point in my life, I choose peace, progression, and purpose over potential that never moves.

✦

I wasted a whole lot of my fifties still involving myself with my baby girls father. He was the only one man I couldn't seem to cast aside as easily as the others. I love my youngest daughter's father deeply, but due to his history of street life and unresolved trauma, he was incapable of loving me in the way I deserved. His personality was difficult and self-focused, and because of that, marriage was never something I truly wanted with him. Still, I did desire a deeper bond, especially because we shared a child. I wanted him to be a good man without an ulterior motive, simply because it was the right thing to be.

Phill and I were friends for nearly twenty years, long before our daughter, Journey Schy, was ever conceived. In many ways, he was my protector. If anyone ever disrespected me or my salon, he was the person I would call. He carried a reputation that came from having power and respect in the streets, particularly in the neighborhood where my braid shop was located. When we are young and still finding ourselves, that kind of edge can feel exciting or even comforting. At one point in my life, I interpreted it as strength.

As I grew older, especially into my forties and fifties, that same energy no longer felt attractive or reassuring. Although he was no longer actively involved in street life, a reputation like that tends to follow a person indefinitely. With maturity came clarity, and I realized that what once felt like protection no longer aligned with the kind of emotional safety I desired.

I believe his past robbed him of some of the emotional tools necessary for a healthy, loving partnership. Many of his actions felt calculated, more rooted in self-preservation and control than in genuine connection. The life he chose made him guarded and, at times, emotionally unavailable. I always knew I deserved more than that, even from someone I loved.

I longed for a kinder, more attentive presence in my life. I wanted a man who was naturally protective and thoughtful, someone who checked to see if I made it home safely, who called to ask if I or my children needed anything. I desired a loving, emotionally present partner, and that simply was not who he was capable of being at the time.

Apologies were rare. Instead of addressing conflict, he allowed time to pass and hoped it would dissolve on its own. Communication, something I value deeply, was consistently lacking. Healthy communication was at the top of my list of qualities I wanted in a partner. Looking back, I have no doubt that continuing to re-involve myself with him delayed the entrance of the man God truly had for me.

Before I was ready to fully sever that soul tie, I tried a different approach. Rather than focusing on everything I felt he lacked, I began to soften my own heart and develop compassion for what had been taken from him emotionally. I convinced myself that somewhere beneath the layers of pain and defense was a better version of him.

That belief caused me to develop a deeper, but different, kind of love. I fell in love with the idea of who I thought he could be. After knowing him for over twenty-five years and sharing a child, it felt painful to accept that I had never truly experienced the best of him. Our daughter has one of the sweetest, most loving spirits I have ever seen, and I believed some of that goodness had to come from him as well. The hope that one day I would meet a more emotionally evolved version of him kept me connected far longer than I should have been.

I know it may sound like I was making excuses for him. I've had that same conversation with myself. I, too, had a difficult upbringing, yet I chose kindness and growth. We all have choices. Still, I wanted to have a better story to tell our daughter. I wanted the positive memories to be real, not something I had to invent later to protect her heart. So I kept reigniting what should have been allowed to fade.

There were moments when things felt lighter, moments where I believed there was hope. But one thing I have learned is that accepting only pieces of someone is not love. Once self-esteem is fully developed, we understand we deserve consistency, kindness, and emotional safety all of the time, not just in fragments.

My family and friends were less forgiving. They grew tired of watching me hold onto hope and paint a picture that did not align with reality. My older children struggled to understand how I could forgive his inconsistency as a father. The truth is, I believed he would change. I believed he would become the man he presented himself as publicly. I believed growth would come naturally with time.

I prayed. I visualized. I believed deeply in the power of transformation. While I still believe those practices can influence outcomes, I never wanted to force change on him. I wanted growth to come from within. It didn't.

Eventually, I reached a point where hope alone was no longer enough. I knew I did not have to accept the emotional weight of his unresolved wounds. While our physical connection remained intense and often confusing, I also knew I did not want a future with him. I did not want permanence. I wanted respect, emotional clarity, and peace.

I was relieved that it was not my responsibility to heal him. I didn't have the energy to dismantle his defenses or endure cycles that never resolved. Still, our physical connection persisted as intensely as ever, blurring boundaries and keeping the attachment alive longer than it should have. I told myself I was fine with it, but deep down, I continued to crave emotional depth.

I uplifted him. I respected him. I focused on his strengths, especially for our daughter's sake. I wanted her to see her father through a lens of dignity and possibility. I hoped my example of kindness and emotional growth would inspire something similar in him.

Make no mistake, I know my worth. That understanding took years of inner work and self-reflection. My self-esteem became the boundary that ultimately protected me. It kept me from being consumed by someone who, intentionally or not, benefited from imbalance.

I knew I was confident, capable, and accomplished. Still, there were moments when his withholding of affirmation made me question myself. That realization was painful, but necessary. It helped me see how subtle emotional dynamics can slowly erode even the strongest spirit.

I was exhausted by the cycle. I wanted to understand him on a deeper level, but I finally accepted that not everyone is ready or willing to explore their inner world. As I continued to grow spiritually, I desired spiritual connection. He was not ready for that space, and that was something I could no longer ignore.

I share this story transparently because I know I am not alone. Healing is not linear. Even after significant growth, old attachments can resurface. That does not mean failure. It means there is still something to learn.

Eventually, I was ready to move forward completely. I released the bond and chose to allow our connection to exist only in the role that mattered most, as parents. I stopped waiting for an apology. I stopped waiting for change. I trusted that God had already given me the clarity I needed.

Then came the experience that confirmed everything.

One evening, after once again engaging physically with my daughter's father, I felt an overwhelming sense of emotional and spiritual discomfort. This time felt different. My soul felt unsettled, as though I had stepped away from my path. That feeling followed me home and lingered.

Later that night, something occurred that I still cannot fully explain. I was not asleep. I was conscious, aware, and present. What I experienced felt like a spiritual vision, though I hesitate to label it definitively. What unfolded felt symbolic, emotional, and deeply personal.

The imagery, the sensation, the clarity of awareness all reinforced one truth. This connection was no longer aligned with my spirit. A Literal spirit came into my bedroom and told me to leave him alone. Whether it was a warning, a release, or a lesson completing itself, I cannot say. But it marked a turning point for me.

That experience confirmed for me that there is a spiritual realm beyond what we understand. It reinforced that not every attachment is meant to last forever, even when love exists.

Today, our daughter is growing beautifully, and her father has made strides in his own journey. He has become a better parent and found ways to use his voice to guide others away from the path he once walked. That growth matters. It deserves acknowledgment.

We now interact with mutual respect and purpose. Our past does not define our present. We both carry wounds, but we also carry the ability to heal. I believe our paths crossed for a reason. For lessons maybe. For growth and transformation. Or maybe to bring our beautiful little girl into the world.

Love is powerful. Love heals. Love softens. Love teaches. Love, when rooted in wisdom, knows when to release.

No matter who we once were or what we endured, we are always capable of returning to our truest nature. Kindness. Growth. Love.

And that is the story I want my daughter to read one day.

7

When Drama Stops Being Attractive

In 2023, I essentially became a serial dater. I liked to exchange numbers quickly and meet up even quicker. I didn't want to waste time bonding with someone I wasn't sure I'd have any chemistry with. When I was in the mood to meet a man, I would prepare myself for the long, extended conversations that people usually have when getting to know each other. I would log onto one of the Internet dating websites and take it from there. But because I was always trying to fix myself and fully heal all past wounds and old toxic behaviors, I couldn't help but notice the universal need we all have to be applauded and complemented by others. It wasn't just me.

One of the guys I dated would constantly ask questions like, "So, what do you think of me?" After our first kiss, he asked, "How was the kiss? Did you feel any spark?"

I'm never one to deny anyone a compliment, but some questions I would never ask because they reflect extreme insecurity. I learned two lessons from dealing with this particular person: no matter how intelligent or powerful a man may be, he still needs reassurance. Even if I got annoyed with him for draining me of every compliment he could, I had to realize that I, too, required the same validation. Maybe not as much, but I still wanted an acknowledgment of my value and beauty. Realizing this made me more compassionate and patient with his constant need for validation. I'm so proud of myself for reaching a point in my life where I can internalize things first. I look inside and see which behaviors actually mirror my own personality traits. Many things that annoy us in others are things we're also guilty of. I use that self- assessment to grow as a person. There is a fine line between enjoying accolades and compliments and crucially needing validation from others. Yes, it feels great to be told you're attractive, successful, and appreciated by others, but being able to do that for yourself feels even better.

I truly enjoyed filling this book with stories of how I found the positive in everyday situations. One day, I was meeting a guy I connected with on Plenty of Fish, an Internet dating website. This would be our first time seeing each other in person after a couple of brief telephone conversations. At this stage in my life, I was interested in dating and open to entering a long-term relationship.

✦

When I had time, I would meet a guy for breakfast, lunch, or dinner to see if we had any chemistry. On this particular day, I was meeting a guy at a popular breakfast restaurant, Roscoe's Chicken and Waffles. On my drive there, he called and said he had a funny story to tell me when I arrived. When I got there, I immediately walked over to the table where he was sitting. He stood up to greet me, and the first thing I noticed was that he was sweating profusely through his shirt. I had brought a copy of one of my books because when he found out I was an author, he said he wanted to purchase a book from me. We sat down, and I took my book out of my purse, placed it on the table, and slid it in his direction. He glanced down at it, then smiled and began telling me the funny story he had mentioned earlier.

He started laughing and said, "You're not going to believe this."

I said, "What happened?" He said that when he was leaving his home to meet me for breakfast, he thought he grabbed his wallet, but he didn't. I was not in the least bit amused. He went on to say, "If you pay for breakfast, I'll pay you back later today via Zelle or CashApp." At that point, I realized I was being played and that he was attempting to scam me into paying for the meal. I said, "Why didn't you simply call me and say you'd be a little late because you had to turn around and go back home to retrieve your wallet?" He had no logical answer, so I stood up and said, "I see this is a game you play with women. You're way too old for this. I'm leaving."

He then said, "You're going to let this make you miss out on a good man?" I laughed out loud, took my book off the table, and walked toward the front door. He started following me. Every part of me wanted to turn around and tell all the waiters, waitresses, and security guard that he was a scam artist and not allow him back into the restaurant. However, I didn't want to make a scene, so I didn't say a word. I wanted to scream, "This fool just tried to play me for a meal."

I'm big on controlling my reactions, so I walked out of the restaurant in complete silence. He followed me out, saying something I couldn't comprehend because I had tuned him out. I walked to my car, got inside, and sat there for a minute or two. It's not easy to take the high road when you feel that someone is trying to take advantage of you. I took a few deep breaths,

66

applauded myself for not acting foolishly in the restaurant, and suddenly realized I was still very hungry. Once I was sure he was gone, I got back out of my car and went back inside. I had decided to treat myself to breakfast. The waitress sat me at the same table where he and I had sat. As I was preparing to order, I caught the eye of a woman sitting at an adjacent table. She smiled and said, "I wasn't trying to be nosy, but I saw and heard what just happened with that guy." I smiled and went over to sit with her at her table.

We laughed and enjoyed breakfast together. When it was time to pay, I said, "I will gladly pay for your food before I allow someone to manipulate me with the lie of forgetting his wallet." She was very gracious. We traded more laughs and shared dating stories, talking about how difficult it was to date in our fifties. She turned out to be a really nice person, so we exchanged numbers and discussed cultivating a new friendship.

There is always something positive in every situation. Had I publicly humiliated the man and made a loud scene in the restaurant, I wouldn't have felt good about responding that way. In life, when we take the time to breathe, sit back, and assess a situation before reacting impulsively, it's always a better option. Rather than focus on the trickster of a man and the negativity of it all, I chose to honor myself and respond in a way I could be proud of. In the end, I met a wonderful person and built a lifelong friendship.

◆

In early 2024, I was dating a tall, dark-skinned man from Los Angeles name Ven who coached basketball at a nearby high school. We went on several dates, and they were all pleasant. Although we didn't have the deep, stimulating conversations I love, he had a beautiful smile, was generous, and didn't mind driving and paying for dinner. He was affectionate, and we seemed to have great physical chemistry. He didn't pressure me for an intimate connection, but eventually, one evening after dinner, we went back to his apartment and had sex. He lived in a tiny one-bedroom apartment with a big boxer dog. After approximately three minutes of intimacy, he fell fast asleep, leaving me awake to entertain the dog. The sex was horrible and quick, and for a few moments, it seemed like he had forgotten how to make love to a woman. He had been drinking quite a bit, which hadn't initially concerned me, until I remembered that he had to drive me home. He never woke up on his own, so after about an hour, I got up, dressed, and shook him fiercely until he finally came back to life. He got up, took another sip of alcohol, and found his keys to take me home.

I was beyond irritated that he was drinking more alcohol as we left, knowing he had to drive. I said, "Hey, hey, stop drinking, sir. You have to drive me home." He dismissed my concerns, and we got in the car. He drove recklessly and too fast, and when I complained, he drove even faster, laughing as if it were funny to scare me with his bad driving. Fortunately, I made it home safely.

The next day, he called, and I told him how irresponsible he had been. I didn't even mention the horrible three minutes of sex. The reason I held back initially was that I was truly trying to work on that lingering part of my personality that would express my feelings, even if it hurt someone. So, I didn't bring it up at all. We had a few more conversations where he boasted about our "great" sex. I was mortified.

I tried to give him a chance to redeem himself, so I came over once more. While he was in the kitchen, I asked him a simple, random question, and he snapped at me in a very rude way. When I came out of the bathroom he was standing near the stove. While walking towards him, I playfully asked, "Hey what are you cooking?" He snapped and said "Girl go sit your ass down and stop following me around my house." He instantly noticed my energy shift and ran over to apologize, but I was too stunned. I sat down for a minute; he apologized again, but I told him I wanted to leave. He walked me out in silence, and I could see he felt bad. However, the quick switch in his personality concerned me. It led me to believe that the person who just snapped at me was who he really was, possibly the nice man who liked to take me to dinner was an impostor.

Now I knew it was wrong to tell this man that he was a horrible lover, and I didn't say it in that cruel way. However, I did let him know how disappointed I was with his rude behavior and irresponsible drunk driving. I also told him that I was shocked he was satisfied with our sexual encounter because I certainly was not.

Now, I realize I could have left that out, and I struggled with myself because I could have easily just moved on without alluding to the fact that he was a horrible lover. I also know that if he had not snapped at me that evening, I might have never said anything.

The point of sharing this story with you is this: No matter who you are or how much work you have done to be a positive person, each day and in each circumstance, you still have to choose to stay positive. However, we are humans and still susceptible to the pressures of life. We don't always make the right choices, and sometimes we give into negative behaviors. I technically failed that time, I could have made a different choice. I could have kept all of that to myself. I was well aware that what I was saying could be hurtful, and I would not want someone to do that to me.

However, even if you don't agree, I still feel I grew in this situation because I acknowledged that I could have been kinder. I didn't say anything for two days because I had an internal battle with myself, and I lost the battle. Yes, he was a jerk for snapping at me, yes, he put my life in danger with his unsafe driving, and yes, he was the worst lover ever, but I could have communicated that to him in a kinder way, or not at all.

What I love about myself is that I am at a point in my life where I always check myself. I constantly acknowledge how I can be a better person. I do not always make the right choices, but I truly believe growth and change begin with acknowledgment. I am not saying I did some horrible thing to this man; I am simply saying I could have just left him alone and spared his feelings. I could have let the next woman deal with his ego. Yes, I lost the battle that time, but I am still very much a work in progress.

The ultimate goal for me is to avoid unleashing words or actions that don't come from a place of love. My goal is to be "Perfectly Positive" the next time around, to control the urge to say something unkind, even if it's based on truth. Just because something is true does not mean it needs to be spoken aloud. Or maybe I'll do some mental creative visualization and manifest the perfect mate so there won't be a next time.

I'm not perfect, and neither are you. The idea is to choose the kinder option when you find yourself in situations like these. The moral of that particular story is this: always stop, think, and try to come from a place of love, even if the other person did not give you the same consideration. We don't want to leave scars on people intentionally. Try to avoid causing anyone unnecessary pain. Fight the urge to speak your mind and tell people off, especially when you are angry or hurt. No good comes from it. Yes, there are important conversations that need to be had at times, but always enter those conversations calmly and compassionately.

If you make mistakes like I did in that situation, apologize quickly if the opportunity allows, and don't beat yourself up about it. You, too, deserve grace and love on this beautiful journey of life. Each day you awaken with air in your lungs, you have another opportunity to make things right. True growth is recognizing when you need to. I didn't always make the right choices, but I was determined to fully understand why I had the urge to cut the men's egos down as I exited the relationship. I knew that trait came from an unhealed place, and I'm still on a journey of healing.

Growth is a process, so be loving and patient with yourself, and never give up on becoming the best version of yourself. Returning to our true nature of love is the ultimate mission. I am so grateful to be on that amazing path, but it definitely comes with a moral meter. Take responsibility when you are wrong. Learn to treat others exactly how you want to be treated. On this path to positivity, you will learn to master transcending the ego. Yes, our feelings get hurt, and sometimes our behavior responds negatively to that hurt, but each time you choose kindness over cruelty, each time you choose love over hate, you are evolving. I wish that for us all.

✦

8

Maybe it's the Lion in Me

Fortunately, I have never been the type of woman to financially support a man. Maybe it's the Leo in me. I have always been a lion through and through. I may have had my heart broken, but never my wallet. That part of me was never negotiable. No one ever sat me down and told me not to give men money. It wasn't taught. It was instinctive. Something in me always knew that love and financial responsibility were not meant to flow in that direction.

I was raised old school. Men paid the bills, and women never reached into their purses. My mother, my grandmother, and the women before me moved through the world with a certain understanding. A man showed his care through provision, and a woman showed hers through support, nurturing, and partnership. While I understand that times have changed, and many women now earn just as much or more than men, there are still some core values I am not willing to abandon.

What I am not okay with is a man who expects money from a woman. I am not comfortable with men who want companion-ship, access, and benefits without being in a position to sustain themselves. Dating costs money. Life costs money. And if a man is not financially stable enough to date, then he is simply not ready to date. That may sound harsh, but it is honest.

Make no mistake, I am far from unfair. I am generous by nature. If a man takes me out, treats me with respect, and consistently shows up as a gentleman, I have no issue offering to take him out in return and paying the entire bill. I enjoy doing that when it feels reciprocal and balanced. What I will not do is become someone's solution, safety net, or financial backup plan disguised as romance.

The issue I have noticed, especially dating over fifty, is that too many men are operating from a place of entitlement instead of pride. They want a woman, but they do not want the responsibility that comes with being a partner. They want companionship, but they are not prepared to contribute equally, emotionally or financially. Somewhere along the way, pride slipped out the window.

When I look back at our grandfathers, I cannot help but notice the difference. Those men worked hard, often with far fewer opportunities, yet they carried themselves with dignity. They may not have had much, but what they had, they took pride in. They did not look to women to rescue them. They did not confuse romance with dependency.

Today, I see too many grown men who are comfortable asking women for money, help, favors, or access they have not earned. That is not strength to me. That is not partnership. And it certainly is not attractive.

Maybe it really is the lion in me. Lions do not hunt in reverse. They do not apologize for their standards. They do not diminish themselves to make others feel comfortable. I have worked too hard, healed too deeply, and learned too much to play small or pretend that imbalance is love.

At this stage in my life, I am not looking for someone to take care of me, but I am also not looking to take care of someone else. I want a partner, not a project. I want mutual effort, mutual respect, and mutual responsibility. Anything less is not dating. It is negotiating my worth, and that is something I will never do again.

✦

I had an intense involvement with a man named Gil, whom I initially hired to coach me. Once again, I found myself drawn to a man in a position of power. Maybe it is the Lion in me. We shared similar career goals, but he had far surpassed me professionally, and that impressed me. I hired him to assist me in reaching my own goals, but the chemistry between us was immediate and undeniable.

He was from the same city I grew up in, and he had the most beautiful skin. What truly captivated me, though, was that he had something to say. I am deeply attracted to a man with strong opinions and the ability to engage in stimulating conversation across many subjects. When that level of intellectual connection is paired with powerful physical chemistry, it creates an undeniable intensity.

The Leo in me enjoyed every bit of it. He was always working, but we made time to connect in person whenever he was in town. I felt comfortable with him in a way that felt both grounding and exciting. I do not take advice easily, but his was different. His guidance mattered to me, and I took it seriously. He was instrumental in pushing me to complete my first book, *My Spiritual Smile: Tools for Mental and Emotional Transformation,* and I will always be grateful to him for that.

We shared many dinners filled with meaningful conversation, laughter, and insight. Even so, he was far too busy to offer the consistency I needed on a full-time basis. Still, I grew to have a deep love and respect for him. I would not trade the time we shared for anything. As an alpha Leo woman, I am aware that my strength can intimidate many men. Gil was not intimidated at all, and that confidence was incredibly attractive to me.

He was present in my life during one of my most vulnerable seasons, the time when my biological mother passed away. His support helped me stay emotionally grounded and focused on the vision I had set for myself as an author and speaker. During a period when it would have been easy to lose direction, he helped me maintain momentum and purpose. For that alone, I hold immense respect for him.

I have no regrets about our connection. The chemistry we shared was rare, the kind that does not come around often. When that type of connection is paired with a brilliant, driven man who genuinely wants to see you succeed, it leaves a lasting impression. Even so, I do not believe relationships like that are always meant to last forever. Two strong leaders who are both accustomed to steering the ship can enjoy one another deeply, but only for a season.

There comes a point when balance matters more than intensity. Two powerful forces can inspire one another, but they can also exhaust each other if neither is willing to yield. That realization did not diminish what we had. It simply clarified what it was. I will always wish him the best, and he will always hold a special place in my heart because he was one of the rare men who truly wanted to see me win.

Not every encounter is meant to become a long-term relationship. Some people enter our lives to elevate us, sharpen us, and prepare us for the next level. When that advancement comes with great food, rich conversations filled with wisdom, and undeniable chemistry, it can still be a gift, even if it is temporary. I have learned to honor those connections for what they are, appreciate them fully, and release them without regret.

9

Love Isn't Over, It's Just Evolved

There comes a point in life when you realize that love did not fail you. Life didn't cheat you. You didn't miss your moment. What actually happened is that *you grew.* Your standards matured. Your nervous system calmed. Your heart became wiser, and once that happens, the way you approach love can never be the same again.

This chapter is not about rules. It is not about strategies or checklists. It is about perspective. It is about learning how to date without fear, without bitterness, and without dragging old wounds into new experiences. It is about approaching love with lightness instead of pressure, curiosity instead of control, and hope instead of exhaustion.

If you are reading this, chances are you have lived, loved and lost. You have tolerated too much, waited too long, and healed more deeply than anyone will ever truly understand. That alone makes you powerful. That alone makes you worthy of love that feels safe, joyful, and aligned.

Dating later in life requires a different posture. You are no longer auditioning for approval. You are not trying to prove your value. You are not desperate to be chosen. You are doing the *choosing*. That shift alone changes everything.

One of the greatest lessons I've learned is that emotional control is not about being guarded. It is about being intentional. It is the ability to observe without reacting, to listen without projecting, and to disengage without drama. When you control your emotions, you stop taking everything personally. You stop assigning meaning too quickly. You also stop confusing attention with intention.

That is when dating becomes lighter. Lighthearted dating does not mean careless dating. It means releasing unrealistic expectations. It means allowing people to show you who they are over time instead of rushing to label the connection. You can enjoy conversations without mentally planning a future that has not yet been earned.

So many women walk into dating carrying invisible weight. The weight of past disappointment and heartbreak. The weight of time lost. That weight shows up as tension, hypervigilance, and emotional fatigue. Love cannot breathe under that pressure.

You are allowed to laugh again. You are allowed to flirt again. You are allowed to explore connection without immediately asking, "Is this my husband?" You are allowed to enjoy a date for what it is, not what it might become.

Being open does not mean being naive. It means being present. It means listening without judgment. It means understanding that people come from different backgrounds, different emotional skill sets, and different stages of healing. Openness is not ignoring red flags. It is not shrinking boundaries. It is simply approaching people as human instead of as threats.

Judgment is often a defense mechanism. We judge to protect ourselves from disappointment. We criticize to avoid vulnerability. We dismiss people quickly so we do not have to sit with uncertainty. While discernment is necessary, harsh judgment closes doors that curiosity could have gently opened.

Some of the most meaningful connections do not arrive packaged the way we imagined. They arrive quietly. Unexpectedly. Sometimes awkwardly. Sometimes imperfectly. Modern dating reflects modern life, fast-paced, digital, diverse, and unconventional. Resisting it only creates frustration.

Online dating, apps, speed dating, social groups, meetups, these are not signs that love has become shallow. They are signs that connection has expanded. Love now has more doorways than ever before. The key is learning how to walk through those doors without losing yourself.

Speed dating might sound intimidating, but it can also be refreshing. It removes the pressure of performance. It forces presence. It invites spontaneity. You learn quickly who feels comfortable, who listens, who engages. You don't have time to overthink. You simply show up as yourself.

Modern dating invites flexibility. It asks you to release rigid ideas about how love "should" arrive. Love does not need candlelight and destiny-level drama to be real. Sometimes it begins with laughter over coffee, a shared interest, or an unexpected conversation.

Giving up on love is easy. Staying open takes courage. There is a difference between protecting your heart and closing it. Protection is calm. Closure is rigid. Protection allows connection to flow with boundaries. Closure blocks it entirely. When you shut down emotionally, you do not just keep pain out, you keep joy out too.

You do not need to relive old stories. You do not need to prove resilience. You do not need to test people. You need to experience

79

them. You need to let moments be moments. One of the most freeing realizations is understanding that not every date needs to lead somewhere. Some dates exist to remind you that you are interesting. Some exist to sharpen your discernment. Some exist to heal old narratives. Some exist to make you laugh. That does not make them failures.

Love does not respond well to desperation or rigidity. It responds to ease. When you control your emotions, you stop chasing outcomes. You stop forcing chemistry. You stop overlooking misalignment just to feel chosen. You allow things to unfold. You trust yourself enough to walk away without collapsing emotionally.

This is where maturity shows up. You no longer confuse excitement with compatibility. You no longer mistake chaos for passion. You no longer tolerate inconsistency just to feel desired. You also stop punishing new people for what old people did. That is very important.

Every man you meet is not responsible for your past heartbreak. Every woman you meet is not obligated to heal your wounds. Dating with emotional control means staying in the present. It means responding to what is happening now, not reacting to what happened before.

You are allowed to want love. You are allowed to want companionship. You are allowed to want intimacy, laughter, touch, and shared experiences. Desire does not make you weak. Wanting connection does not mean you have failed at independence. You can be whole and still want partnership. As women, we are often taught to either sacrifice ourselves for love or reject it entirely. There is a middle ground. That middle ground is self-respect. It is softness with strength. It is openness with boundaries.

Lighthearted dating invites joy back into the process. It reminds you that attraction can be playful. That conversation can be stimulating. That chemistry does not have to be chaotic to be real. Let go of the idea that love must look a certain way by a certain age. Love does not follow timelines. It follows readiness. Some people meet the love of their life at twenty-five. Some at forty-five. Some at sixty-five. Some more than once. Love does not diminish with age. It deepens.

Your heart has not expired. Your story is not over. You are not "too much," "too late," or "too set in your ways." You are seasoned. You are self-aware. You are capable of discerning without dismissing.

Dating becomes more enjoyable when you remove the pressure to win or lose. There is no scoreboard. There is only experience. You either learn, grow, or connect. All three are valuable. If love arrives, receive it. If it does not, keep living fully. Do not put your life on hold waiting for a relationship to validate it.

The most attractive energy is someone who is at peace with themselves. Try something new. Say yes to a different kind of date. Step outside your usual type. Laugh at the awkward moments. Release the need to control the outcome. Allow yourself to be surprised.

Modern love is not less meaningful. It is simply more honest. People are showing you who they are faster. Emotional maturity is more visible. Red flags appear sooner. That is a gift if you are paying attention. Do not give up on love because it did not arrive the way you expected. Do not close your heart because someone mishandled it. Do not confuse caution with fear.

Love is still here. It is just asking you to meet it with wisdom instead of wounds, curiosity instead of judgment, and emotional control instead of emotional exhaustion.

If you can do that, love will find you. And when it does, it will feel lighter than anything you have ever known.

Because love did not fail you. It evolved, and so did you.

About the Author

SaBrina Fisher Reece is a woman whose life reflects resilience, reinvention, and the transformative power of self-awareness. For over twenty-six years, she was known throughout California as "The Braid Queen," the visionary behind *Braids By SaBrina*, the legendary salon and school on Adams Boulevard that became one of the most influential braiding institutions in Los Angeles. What she built was more than a business; it was a community rooted in confidence, creativity, and empowerment.

As SaBrina entered a new season of life, she felt a deeper calling to help others navigate emotional growth, personal healing, and conscious living. That calling expanded into writing and speaking, where she shares candid life experiences and practical wisdom that guide people toward clarity, self-respect, and inner peace.

In *Over 50 and Still Fine Looking to Date Again*, SaBrina brings her signature honesty and insight to modern dating, offering real-life stories and emotional lessons for men and women navigating love later in life. With humor, compassion, and discernment, she encourages readers to date with confidence, control their emotions, recognize red flags, and remain open to love without compromising their peace.

She is also the author of *My Spiritual Smile, Living Life on a Higher Frequency, Perfectly Positive, Sexuality & Spirituality: Unlocking the Sacred Power Between Body & Soul,* and *Your Mind Is Magic.* Across all her work, SaBrina reminds readers that transformation begins within and that emotional intelligence is the foundation for a fulfilling life.

SaBrina is a devoted mother of four and a proud grandmother. Her greatest joy is witnessing others awaken to the truth that their minds, choices, and boundaries are their most powerful tools.

Her message is simple, honest, and life-changing:
Your mind is magic. Use it with intention.

You can connect with me on:
⊕ https://in59secondspublishing.com

Also by SaBrina Fisher Reece

SaBrina Fisher Reece's body of work spans personal development, spirituality, emotional wellness, and entrepreneurship. Her books provide clear guidance on mindset mastery, faith-based manifestation, positive identity, effective prayer, emotional balance, sexual-spiritual harmony, and the fundamentals of building and sustaining a small business. Together, her titles offer a comprehensive blueprint for improving both inner life and external success, making her an author dedicated to empowering readers on every level: spiritual, emotional, mental, and practical.

PROFOUND

Profound: Ancient Wisdom that Changed My Life

This series was not written to convince you of anything.

It was written to remind you of something.

For most of my life, I searched for answers the same way many people do. I looked outward. I prayed, studied, worked, endured, and tried to become better by force. I believed growth meant effort alone and that transformation required suffering. I was taught, as many of us are, what to believe, what to question, and what to avoid.

What I did not realize at the time was that I was not missing faith.

I was missing understanding.

The *Profound Series* was born from a deeply personal journey of self-discovery, healing, and expansion. It is the result of decades of reading ancient texts, studying metaphysical teachings, reflecting on spiritual principles, and most importantly, applying this wisdom in real life. This series is not meant to replace religion, tradition, or belief systems. It is meant to widen the lens.

Religion offers structure, community, and devotion. Ancient wisdom offers context, depth, and responsibility. Together, they reveal something powerful: that you are not separate from the divine, and you were never meant to live disconnected from your inner power.

This series exists because I discovered that much of what we are seeking has already been known for centuries. Long before modern psychology, neuroscience, or self-help, ancient philosophers, mystics, teachers, and spiritual scholars under-stood the relationship between thought, emotion, conscious-ness, and reality. They understood that the mind is creative, that belief shapes experience, and that life responds to awareness.

The first book, **Profound**, is about remembering. It is about gathering ancient wisdom and recognizing truths that may feel familiar even if you are encountering them for the first time. This is the awakening stage. The moment when something inside you says, "There is more."

The second book, **Activate**, is about embodiment. Knowledge alone does not change a life. It must be practiced. This book moves wisdom from the intellect into daily living. It teaches you how to tap into the divine energy within you and apply what you have learned in practical, grounded ways.

The third book, **Think**, is about mastery of the mind. Thought is not passive. It is creative. This book guides you in becoming aware of your inner dialogue, understanding how thoughts shape experience, and learning how to consciously direct the mental patterns that influence your life.

The fourth book, **Live**, is about integration. This is where knowledge, practice, and awareness become who you are. You no longer strive to be aligned. You live aligned. You move through the world with clarity, compassion, and confidence, embodying the wisdom you have gained.

Together, these four books form a complete journey.

Awakening. Activation. Mastery. Expression.

This is not a quick fix. It is not spiritual bypassing. It is not about perfection. It is about responsibility. Responsibility for your thoughts. Responsibility for your emotional state. Responsibility for the energy you bring into the world.

The world does not need more information. It needs more

conscious people. People who are self-aware. People who understand cause and effect at the level of thought and emotion. People who can pause, reflect, and respond instead of react. People who live from inner alignment rather than fear.

You were never meant to live small, disconnected, or power-less. You were meant to participate in your own evolution.

This series is an invitation. Not to abandon what you believe, but to expand it. Not to follow me, but to follow your own inner knowing. Not to search endlessly outside yourself, but to reconnect with what has always been within you.

If you are reading this, you are ready.

Ready to remember.

Ready to activate.

Ready to master your mind.

Ready to live fully.

Welcome to the journey.

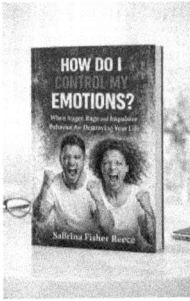

How Do I Control My Emotions?

How Do I Control My Emotions?

When Anger, Rage, and Impulsive Behavior Is Destroying Your Life

Anger does not make you powerful. It makes you reactive. And unchecked reactions can quietly dismantle your relationships, your health, your career, and your peace.

In **How Do I Control My Emotions?**, author and transformational voice **SaBrina Fisher Reece** takes you on a deeply honest journey through emotional self-mastery. Drawing from her own lived experiences as a business owner, leader, and woman who once wore anger as armor, SaBrina exposes the real roots of rage, impulsive behavior, and emotional outbursts—and shows you how to take your power back.

This book is not about suppressing emotions or pretending everything is fine. It is about understanding why you react the way you do, identifying hidden triggers tied to abandonment, trauma, and unmet needs, and learning how to pause, choose, and respond with intention instead of regret.

Inside these pages, you will learn:

Why anger feels justified in the moment but costs you in the long run

How unhealed pain disguises itself as control, dominance, or intensity

The difference between reacting and responding

Why emotional discipline is a form of self-respect

How to stop letting your past control your present

Written with compassion, clarity, and accountability, this book is a call to action for anyone tired of apologizing, repairing damage, or living with the consequences of emotional explosions. If you are ready to stop being ruled by anger and start living from self-control, awareness, and peace, this book will meet you exactly where you are.

You cannot control other people.

But you can always control **you**.

And that changes everything.

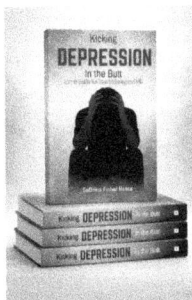

Kicking Depression in the Butt

Kicking Depression in the Butt: How to Battle the Internal enemy and Win. is a raw, faith-infused, and deeply practical guide for anyone who is tired of surviving in silence and ready to reclaim their life.

Drawing from her own lived experiences with trauma, abandonment, loss, and depression, SaBrina Fisher Reece invites readers into an honest conversation about what depression really feels like, and how to fight back. This book does not minimize pain or offer shallow positivity. Instead, it helps readers recognize depression as an internal enemy, interrupt destructive thought cycles, and rebuild their inner world with intention, truth, and daily tools that actually work.

Through personal storytelling, spiritual insight, and mindset-shifting strategies, SaBrina shows readers how to stop identifying with their darkest thoughts and begin designing a life that protects their peace. She addresses the realities of trauma, triggers, boundaries, faith, therapy, medication, and personal responsibility, offering a balanced approach that honors both professional support and inner work.

Kicking Depression in the Butt is for the person who keeps showing up while quietly falling apart. It is for those who smile while suffering, who feel strong on the outside but exhausted on the inside. Most of all, it is a reminder that depression may visit, but it does not get to stay, and it does not get to become your identity.

This book is not about perfection. It's about progress. It's about learning how to fight for your mind, your peace, and your future, one thought, one choice, and one day at a time.

Because as long as you have breath in your body, your story is not over, and you still have the power to kick depression in the butt.

Family Fun Night Cookbook

Family Fun Night Cookbook is more than a collection of recipes, it's a simple, joyful way to bring families back together in the kitchen.

Designed for **kids, teens, and young adults**, this cookbook features **60 easy, safe, and family-approved recipes** that turn everyday meals into meaningful moments. Whether your children are little helpers, teenagers learning independence, or young adults home from college for the holidays, these recipes invite everyone to participate, contribute, and connect.

Cooking together builds more than meals. It builds confidence, communication, patience, and teamwork. This book encourages children of all ages to develop life skills while strengthening family bonds through shared experiences. The recipes are intentionally simple, approachable, and fun, making it easy for busy families to slow down and enjoy time together without stress.

Inside, you'll find meals that work for weeknights, weekends, holidays, and family gatherings, recipes that spark conversation, laughter, and a sense of togetherness. Each dish is crafted to be safe and accessible, allowing kids to help in age-appropriate ways while parents feel confident and relaxed.

In a world that moves fast and pulls families in different directions, **Family Fun Night Cookbook** creates space for connection. It turns cooking into collaboration. It transforms the kitchen into a place of learning, love, and lasting memories.

This is not about perfection. It's about presence.

It's about putting phones down, pulling chairs up, and making memories one recipe at a time.

If you're looking for a simple way to strengthen relationships, teach valuable life skills, and enjoy meaningful time together, this cookbook belongs in your home.